INDEX.

AN

ACCOUNT OF THE PROCEEDINGS

ON THE

TRIAL OF

SUSAN B. ANTHONY,

ON THE

Charge of Illegal Voting,

AT THE

PRESIDENTIAL ELECTION IN NOV., 1872,

AND ON THE

TRIAL OF

BEVERLY W. JONES, EDWIN T. MARSH AND WILLIAM B. HALL,

THE INSPECTORS OF ELECTION BY WHOM HER VOTE WAS RECEIVED.

ROCHESTER, N. Y.:
DAILY DEMOCRAT AND CHRONICLE BOOK PRINT, 3 WEST MAIN ST.
1874.

PREFACE.

At the election of President and Vice President of the United States, and members of Congress, in November, 1872, SUSAN B. ANTHONY, and several other women, offered their votes to the inspectors of election, claiming the right to vote, as among the privileges and immunities secured to them as citizens by the fourteenth amendment to the Constitution of the United States. The inspectors, JONES, HALL, and MARSH, by a majority, decided in favor of receiving the offered votes, against the dissent of HALL, and they were received and deposited in the ballot box. For this act, the women, fourteen in number, were arrested and held to bail, and indictments were found against them severally, under the 19th Section of the Act of Congress of May 30th, 1870, (16 St. at L. 144.) charging them with the offense of "knowingly voting without having a lawful right to vote." The three inspectors were also arrested, but only two of them were held to bail, HALL having been discharged by the Commissioner on whose warrant they were arrested. All three, however were jointly indicted under the same statute—for having "knowingly and wilfully received the votes of persons not entitled to vote."

Of the women voters, the case of Miss ANTHONY alone was brought to trial, a *nolle prosequi* having been entered upon the other indictments. Upon the trial of Miss ANTHONY before the U. S. Circuit Court for the Northern District of New York, at Canandaigua, in June, 1873, it was proved that before offering her vote she was advised by her counsel that she had a right to vote; and that she entertained no doubt, at the time of voting, that she was entitled to vote. It was claimed in her behalf:

I. That she was legally entitled to vote.

II. That if she was not so entitled, but voted in good faith in the belief that it was her right, she was guilty of no crime,

III. That she did vote in such good faith, and with such belief.

The court held that the defendant had no right to vote—that good faith constituted no defence—that there was nothing in the case for the jury to decide, and directed them to find a verdict of guilty; refusing to submit, at the request of the defendant's counsel, any question to the jury, or to allow the clerk to ask the jurors, severally, whether they assented to the verdict which the court had directed to be entered. The verdict of guilty was entered by the clerk, as directed by the court, without any express assent or dissent on the part of the jury. A fine of $100, and costs, was imposed upon the defendant.

Miss ANTHONY insists that in these proceedings, the fundamental principle of criminal law, that no person can be a criminal unless the mind be so—that an honest mistake is not a crime, has been disregarded; that she has been denied her constitutional right of trial by jury, the jury having had no voice in her conviction; that she has been denied her right to have the response of every juror to the question, whether he did or did not assent to the verdict which the court directed the clerk to enter.

The trial of the three inspectors followed that of Miss ANTHONY, and all were convicted, the court holding, as in the case of Miss ANTHONY, that good faith on their part in receiving the votes was not a protection; which they think a somewhat severe rule of law, inasmuch as the statute provides the same penalty, and in the same sentence, "for knowingly and wilfully receiving the vote of any person not entitled to vote, or refusing to receive the vote of any person entitled to vote." The inspectors claim, that according to this exposition of the law, they were placed in a position which required them, without any opportunity to investigate or take advice in regard to the right of any voter whose right was questioned, to decide the question correctly, at the peril of a term in the state's prison if they made a mistake; and, though this may be a correct exposition of the law in their case, they would be sorry to see it applied to the decisions of any court, not excepting the tribunal by which they were convicted.

The defendant, HALL, is at a loss to know how he could have avoided the penalty, inasmuch as he did all that he could in the way of rejecting the votes, without throttling his coinspectors, and forcing them to desist from the wrong of receiving them. He is of opinion that by the ruling of the Court, he would have been equally guilty, if he had tried his strength in that direction, and had failed of success.

To preserve a full record of so important a judicial determination, and to enable the friends of the convicted parties to understand precisely the degree of criminality which attaches to them in consequence of these convictions, the following pamphlet has been prepared—giving a more full and accurate statement of the proceedings than can elsewhere be found.

INDICTMENT

AGAINST SUSAN B. ANTHONY.

DISTRICT COURT OF THE UNITED STATES OF AMERICA,

IN AND FOR THE

NORTHERN DISTRICT OF NEW YORK.

At a stated session of the District Court of the United States of America, held in and for the Northern District of New York, at the City Hall, in the city of Albany, in the said Northern District of New York, on the third Tuesday of January, in the year of our Lord one thousand eight hundred and seventy-three, before the Honorable Nathan K. Hall, Judge of the said Court, assigned to keep the peace of the said United States of America, in and for the said District, and also to hear and determine divers Felonies, Misdemeanors and other offenses against the said United States of America, in the said District committed.

Brace Millerd,
James D. Wasson,
Peter H. Bradt,
James McGinty,
Henry A. Davis,
Loring W. Osborn,
Thomas Whitbeck,
John Mullen,
Samuel G. Harris,
Ralph Davis,
Matthew Fanning,
Abram Kimmey,
Derrick B. Van Schoonhoven,
Wilhelmus Van Natten,
James Kenney,
Adam Winne,
James Goold,
Samuel S. Fowler,
Peter D. R. Johnson,
Patrick Carroll,

good and lawful men of the said District, then and there sworn and charged to inquire for the said United States of America, and for the body of said District, do, upon their oaths, present, that Susan B. Anthony now or late of Rochester, in the county of Monroe, with force and arms, etc., to-wit : at and in the first election district of the eighth ward of the city of Rochester, in the county of Monroe, in said Northern District of New York, and within the jurisdiction of this Court, heretofore, to-wit : on the fifth day of November, in the year of our Lord one thousand eight hundred and seventy-two, at an election duly held at and in the first election district of the said eighth ward of the city of Rochester, in said county, and in said Northern District of New York, which said election was for Representatives in the Congress of the United States, to-wit : a Representative in the Congress of the United States for the State of New York at large, and a Representative in the Congress of the United States for the twenty-ninth Congressional District of the State of New York, said first election district of said eighth ward of said city of Rochester, being then and there a part of said twenty-ninth Congressional District of the State of New York, did knowingly, wrongfully and unlawfully vote for a Representative in the Congress of the United

States for the State of New York at large, and for a Representative in the Congress of the United States for said twenty-ninth Congressional District, without having a lawful right to vote in said election district (the said Susan B. Anthony being then and there a person of the female sex,) as she, the said Susan B. Anthony then and there well knew, contrary to the form of the statute of the United States of America in such case made and provided, and against the peace of the United States of America and their dignity.

Second Count—And the jurors aforesaid upon their oaths aforesaid do further present that said Susan B. Anthony, now or late of Rochester, in the county of Monroe, with force and arms, etc., to-wit: at and in the first election district of the eighth ward of the city of Rochester, in the county of Monroe, in said Northern District of New York, and within the jurisdiction of this Court, heretofore, to-wit: on the fifth day of November, in the year of our Lord one thousand eight hundred and seventy-two, at an election duly held at and in the first election district of the said eighth ward, of said city of Rochester, in said county, and in said Northern District of New York, which said election was for Representatives in the Congress of the United States, to-wit: a Representative in the Congress of the United States for the State of New York at large, and a Representative in the Congress of the United States for the twenty-ninth Congressional District of the State of New York, said first election district of said eighth ward, of said city of Rochester, being then and there a part of said twenty-ninth Congressional District of the State of New York, did knowingly, wrongfully and unlawfully vote for a candidate for Representative in the Congress of the United States for the State of New York at large, and for a candidate for Representative in the Congress of the United States for said twenty-ninth Congressional District, without having a lawful right to vote in said first election district (the said Susan B. Anthony being then and ther a person of the female sex,) as she, the said Susan B. Anthony then and there well knew, contrary to the form of the statute of the United States of America in such case made and provided, and against the peace of the United States of America and their dignity.

RICHARD CROWLEY,
Attorney of the United States,
For the Northern District of New York.

(Endorsed.) Jan. 24, 1873.

Pleads not guilty.

RICHARD CROWLEY,
U. S. Attorney.

UNITED STATES

CIRCUIT COURT.

Northern District of New York.

THE UNITED STATES OF AMERICA

vs.

SUSAN B. ANTHONY.

HON. WARD HUNT, Presiding.

APPEARANCES.

For the United States:

HON. RICHARD CROWLEY.
U. S. District Attorney.

For the Defendant:

HON. HENRY R. SELDEN.
JOHN VAN VOORHIS, ESQ.

Tried at Canandaigua, Tuesday and Wednesday, June 17th and 18th, 1873, before Hon. Ward Hunt, and a jury.

Jury impanneled at 2:30 P. M.

MR. CROWLEY opened the case as follows:

May it please the Court and Gentlemen of the Jury:

On the 5th of November, 1872, there was held in this State, as well as in other States of the Union, a general election for different officers, and among those, for candidates to represent several districts of this State in the Congress of the United States. The defendant, Miss Susan B. Anthony, at that time resided in the city of Rochester, in the county of Monroe, Northern District of New York, and upon the 5th day of November, 1872, she voted for a representative in the Congress of the United States, to represent the 29th Congressional District of this State, and also for a representative at large for the State of New York, to represent the State in the Congress of the United States. At that time she was a woman. I suppose there will be no question about that. The question in this case, if there be a question of fact about it at all, will, in my judgment, be rather a question of law than one of fact. I suppose that there will be no question of fact, substantially, in the case when all of the evidence is out, and it will be for you to decide under the charge of his honor, the Judge, whether or not the defendant committed the offence of voting for a representative in Congress upon that occasion. We think, on the part of the Government, that there is no question about it either one way or the other, neither a question of fact, nor a question of law, and that whatever Miss Anthony's intentions may have been—whether they were good or otherwise—she did not have a right to vote upon that question, and if she did vote without having a lawful right to vote, then there is no question but what she is guilty of violating a law of the United States in that behalf enacted by the Congress of the United States.

We don't claim in this case, gentlemen, that Miss Anthony is of that class of people who go about "repeating." We don't claim that she went from place to place for the purpose of offering her vote. But we do claim that upon the 5th of November, 1872, she voted, and whether she believed that she had a right to vote or not, it being a question of law, that she is within the Statute.

Congress in 1870 passed the following statute: (Reads 19th Section of the Act of 1870, page 144, 16th statutes at large.)

It is not necessary for me, gentlemen, at this stage of the case, to state all the facts which will be proven on the part of the Government. I shall leave that to be shown by the evidence and by the witnesses, and if any question of law shall arise his Honor will undoubtedly give you instructions as he shall deem proper.

Conceded, that on the 5th day of November, 1872, Miss Susan B. Anthony was a woman.

Beverly W. Jones, a witness, called in behalf of the United States, having been duly sworn, testified as follows:

Examined by Mr. Crowley:

Q. Mr. Jones, where do you reside?
A. 8th ward, Rochester.
Q. Where were you living on the 5th of November, 1872?
A. Same place.
Q. Do you know the defendant, Miss Susan B. Anthony?
A. Yes, sir.
Q. In what capacity were you acting upon that day, if any, in relation to elections?
A. Inspector of election.

Q. Into how many election districts is the 8th ward divided, if it contains more than one?

A. Two, sir.

Q. In what election district were you inspector of elections?

A. The first district.

Q. Who were inspectors with you?

A. Edwin T. Marsh and William B. Hall.

Q. Had the Board of Inspectors been regularly organized?

A. Yes, sir.

Q. Upon the 5th day of November, did the defendant, Susan B. Anthony, vote in the first election district of the 8th ward of the city of Rochester?

A. Yes, sir.

Q. Did you see her vote?

A. Yes, sir.

Q. Will you state to the jury what tickets she voted, whether State, Assembly, Congress and Electoral?

Objected to as calling for a conclusion.

Q. State what tickets she voted, it you know, Mr. Jones?

A. If I recollect right she voted the Electoral ticket, Congressional ticket, State ticket, and Assembly ticket.

Q. Was there an election for Member of Congress for that district and for Representative at Large in Congress, for the State of New York, held on the 5th of November, in the city of Rochester?

A. I think there was; yes, sir.

Q. In what Congressional District was the city of Rochester at the time?

A. The 29th.

Q. Did you receive the tickets from Miss Anthony?

A. Yes, sir.

Q. What did you do with them when you received them?

A. Put them in the separate boxes where they belonged.

Q. State to the jury whether you had separate boxes for the several tickets voted in that election district?

A. Yes, sir; we had.

Q. Was Miss Anthony challenged upon that occasion?

A. Yes, sir—no; not on that day she wasn't.

Q. She was not challenged on the day she voted?

A. No, sir.

Cross-Examination by Judge Selden:

Q. Prior to the election, was there a registry of voters in that district made?

A. Yes, sir.

Q. Was you one of the officers engaged in making that registry?

A. Yes, sir.

Q. When the registry was being made did Miss Anthony appear before the Board of Registry and claim to be registered as a voter?

A. She did.

Q. Was there any objection made, or any doubt raised as to her right to vote?

A. There was.

Q. On what ground?

A. On the ground that the Constitution of the State of New York did not allow women to vote.

Q. What was the defect in her right to vote as a citizen?

A. She was not a male citizen.

Q. That she was a woman?

A. Yes, sir.

Q. Did the Board consider that and decide that she was entitled to register?

Objected to. Objection overruled.

Q. Did the Board consider the question of her right to registry, and decide that she was entitled to registry as a voter?

A. Yes, sir.

Q. And she was registered accordingly ?

A. Yes, sir.

Q. When she offered her vote, was the same objection brought up in the Board of Inspectors, or question made of her right to vote as a woman ?

A. She was challenged previous to election day.

Q. It was canvassed previous to election day between them ?

A. Yes, sir ; she was challenged on the second day of registering names.

Q. At the time of the registry, when her name was registered, was the Supervisor of Election present at the Board ?

A. He was.

Q. Was he consulted upon the question of whether she was entitled to registry, or did he express an opinion on the subject to the inspectors ?

MR. CROWLEY : I submit that it is of no consequence whether he did or not.

JUDGE SELDEN : He was the Government Supervisor under this act of Congress.

MR. CROWLEY : The Board of Inspectors, under the State law, constitute the Board of Registry, and they are the only persons to pass upon that question.

THE COURT : You may take it.

A. Yes, sir ; there was a United States Supervisor of Elections, two of them.

By JUDGE SELDEN :

Q. Did they advise the registry, or did they not ?

A. One of them did.

Q. And on that advice the registry was made with the judgment of the inspectors.

A. It had a great deal of weight with the inspectors, I have no doubt.

Re-direct Examination by MR. CROWLEY:

Q. Was Miss Anthony challenged before the Board of Registry?

A. Not at the time she offered her name.

Q. Was she challenged at any time?

A. Yes, sir; the second day of the meeting of the Board.

Q. Was the preliminary and the general oath administered?

A. Yes, sir.

Q. Won't you state what Miss Anthony said, if she said anything, when she came there and offered her name for registration?

A. She stated that she did not claim any rights under the constitution of the State of New York; she claimed her right under the constitution of the United States.

Q. Did she name any particular amendment?

A. Yes, sir; she cited the 14th amendment.

Q. Under that she claimed her right to vote?

A. Yes, sir.

Q. Did the other Federal Supervisor who was present, state it as his opinion that she was entitled to vote under that amendment, or did he protest, claiming that she did not have the right to vote?

A. One of them said that there was no way for the inspectors to get around placing the name upon the register; the other one, when she came in, left the room.

Q. Did this one who said that there was no way to get around placing the name upon the register, state that she had her right to register but did not have the right to vote?

A. I did'nt hear him make any such statement.

Q. You didn't hear any such statement as that?

A. No, sir.

Q. Was there a poll list kept of the voters of the first election district of the 8th ward on the day of election?

A. Yes, sir.

Q. (Handing witness two books,) State whether that is the poll list of voters kept upon the day of election in the first election district of the 8th ward, of the city of Rochester?

A. This is the poll list, and also the register.

Q. Turn to the name of Susan B. Anthony, if it is upon that poll list?

A. I have it.

Q. What number is it?

A. Number 22.

Q. From that poll list what tickets does it purport to show that she voted upon that occasion?

A. Electoral, State, Congress and Assembly.

United States rests.

JUDGE SELDEN opened the case in behalf of the defendant, as follows:

If the Court please, Gentlemen of the Jury:

This is a case of no ordinary magnitude, although many might regard it as one of very little importance. The question whether my client here has done anything to justify her being consigned to a felon's prison or not, is one that interests her very essentially, and that interests the people also essentially. I claim and shall endeavor to establish before you that when she offered to have her name registered as a voter, and when she offered her vote for Member of Congress, she was as much entitled to vote as any man that voted at that election, according to the Constitution and laws of the Government under which she lives. If I maintain that proposition, as a matter of course she has committed no offence, and is entitled to be discharged at your hands.

But, beyond that, whether she was a legal voter or not, whether she was entitled to vote or not, if she sincerely believed that she had a right to vote, and offered her ballot in good faith, under that belief, whether right or wrong, by the laws of this country she is guilty of no crime. I apprehend that that proposition, when it is discussed, will be maintained with a clearness and force that shall leave no doubt upon the mind of the Court or upon your minds as the gentlemen of the jury. If I maintain that proposition here, then the further question and the only question which, in my judgment, can come before you to be passed upon by you as a question of fact is whether or not she did vote in good faith, believing that she had a right to vote.

The public prosecutor assumes that, however honestly she may have offered her vote, however sincerely she may have believed that she had a right to vote, if she was mistaken in that judgment, her offering her vote and its being received makes a criminal offence—a proposition to me most abhorrent, as I believe it will be equally abhorrent to your judgment.

Before the registration, and before this election, Miss Anthony called upon me for advice upon the question whether, under the 14th Amendment of the Constitution of the United States, she had a right to vote. I had not examined the question. I told her I would examine it and give her my opinion upon the question of her legal right. She went away and came again after I had made the examination. I advised her that she was as lawful a voter as I am, or as any other man is, and advised her to go and offer her vote. I may have been mistaken in that, and if I was mistaken, I believe she acted in good faith. I believe she acted according to her right as the law and Constitution gave it to her. But whether she did or not, she acted in the most perfect good faith, and if she made a mistake, or if I made one, that is not a reason for committing her to a felon's cell.

For the second time in my life, in my professional

practice, I am under the necessity of offering myself as a witness for my client.

HENRY R. SELDEN, a witness sworn in behalf of the defendant, testified as follows:

Before the last election, Miss Anthony called upon me for advice, upon the question whether she was or was not a legal voter. I examined the question, and gave her my opinion, unhesitatingly, that the laws and Constitution of the United States, authorized her to vote, as well as they authorize any man to vote; and I advised her to have her name placed upon the registry and to vote at the election, if the inspectors should receive her vote. I gave the advice in good faith, believing it to be accurate, and I believe it to be accurate still.

[This witness was not cross-examined.]

JUDGE SELDEN: I propose to call Miss Anthony as to the fact of her voting— on the question of the intention or belief under which she voted.

MR. CROWLEY: She is not competent as a witness in her own behalf.

[The Court so held.]

Defendant rests.

JOHN E. POUND, a witness sworn in behalf of the United States, testified as follows:

Examined by MR. CROWLEY.

Q. During the months of November and December, 1872, and January, 1873, were you Assistant United States Dist. Attorney for the Northern District of New York?

A. Yes, sir.

Q. Do you know the defendant, Susan B. Anthony?

A. Yes, sir.

Q. Did you attend an examination before Wm. C. Storrs, a United States Commissioner, in the city of Rochester, when her case was examined?

A. I did

Q. Was she called as a witness in her own behalf upon that examination?

A. She was.

Q. Was she sworn?

A. She was.

Q. Did she give evidence?

A. She did.

Q. Did you keep minutes of evidence on that occasion?

A. I did.

Q. (Handing the witness a paper.) Please look at the paper now shown you and see if it contains the minutes you kept upon that occasion?

A. It does.

Q. Turn to the evidence of Susan B. Anthony?

A. I have it.

Q. Did she, upon that occasion, state that she consulted or talked with Judge Henry R. Selden, of Rochester, in relation to her right to vote?

JUDGE SELDEN: I object to that upon the ground that it is incompetent, that if they refuse to allow her to be sworn here, they should be excluded from producing any evidence that she gave elsewhere, especially when they want to give the version which the United States officer took of her evidence.

THE COURT: Go on.

By MR. CROWLEY:

Q. State whether she stated on that examination, under oath, that she had talked or consulted with Judge Henry R. Selden in relation to her right to vote?

A. She did.

Q. State whether she was asked, upon that examination, if the advice given her by Judge Henry R. Selden would or did make any difference in her action in voting, or in substance that?

A. She stated on the cross-examination, "I should have made the same endeavor to vote that I did had I not consulted Judge Selden. I didn't consult any one before I registered. I was not influenced by his advice in the matter at all; have been resolved to vote, the first time I was at home 30 days, for a number of years."

Cross-examination by MR. VAN VOORHEES:

Q. Mr. Pound, was she asked there if she had any doubt about her right to vote, and did she answer "Not a particle?"

A. She stated "Had no doubt as to my right to vote," on the direct examination.

Q. There was a stenographic reporter there, was there not?

A. A reporter was there taking notes.

Q. Was not this question put to her "Did you have any doubt yourself of your right to vote?" and did she not answer "Not a particle?"

THE COURT: Well, he says so, that she had no doubt of her right to vote.

JUDGE SELDEN: I beg leave to state, in regard to my own testimony, Miss Anthony informs me that I was mistaken in the fact that my advice was before her registry. It was my recollection that it was on her way to the registry, but she states to me now that she was registered and came immediately to my office. In that respect I was under a mistake.

Evidence closed.

ARGUMENT OF MR. SELDEN FOR THE DEFENDANT.

The defendant is indicted under the 19th section of the Act of Congress of May 31, 1870 (16 St. at L., 144,), for "voting without having a lawful right to vote."

The words of the Statute, so far as they are material in this case, are as follows:

"If at any election for representative or delegate in the Congress of the United States, any person shall knowingly * * * vote without having a lawful right to vote * * every such person shall be deemed guilty of a crime, * * and on conviction thereof shall be punished by a fine not exceeding $500, or by imprisonment for a term not exceeding three years, or by both, in the discretion of the court, and shall pay the costs of prosecution."

The only alleged ground of illegality of the defendant's vote is that she is a woman. If the same act had been done by her brother under the same circumstances, the act would have been not only innocent, but honorable and laudable; but having been done by a woman it is said to be a crime. The crime therefore consists not in the act done, but in the simple fact that the person doing it was a woman and not a man, I believe this is the first instance in which a woman has been arraigned in a criminal court, merely on account of her sex.

If the advocates of female suffrage had been allowed to choose the point of attack to be made upon their position, they could not have chosen it more favorably for themselves; and I am disposed to thank those who have been instrumental in this proceeding, for presenting it in the form of a criminal prosecution.

Women have the same interest that men have in the establishment and maintenance of good government;

they are to the same extent as men bound to obey the laws; they suffer to the same extent by bad laws, and profit to the same extent by good laws; and upon principles of equal justice, as it would seem, should be allowed equally with men, to express their preference in the choice of law-makers and rulers. But however that may be, no greater *absurdity*, to use no harsher term, could be presented, than that of rewarding men and punishing women, for the same act, *without giving to women any voice in the question which should be rewarded, and which punished.*

I am aware, however, that we are here to be governed by the Constitution and laws as they are, and that if the defendant has been guilty of violating the law, she must submit to the penalty, however unjust or absurd the law may be. But courts are not required to so interpret laws or constitutions as to produce either absurdity or injustice, so long as they are open to a more reasonable interpretation. This must be my excuse for what I design to say in regard to the propriety of female suffrage, because with that propriety established there is very little difficulty in finding sufficient warrant in the constitution for its exercise.

This case, in its legal aspects, presents three questions, which I purpose to discuss.

1. Was the defendant legally entitled to vote at the election in question?

2. If she was not entitled to vote, but believed that she was, and voted in good faith in that belief, did such voting constitute a crime under the statute before referred to?

3. Did the defendant vote in good faith in that belief?

If the first question be decided in accordance with my views, the other questions become immaterial; if the second be decided adversely to my views, the first and third become immaterial. The two first are questions of law to be decided by the court, the other is a question for the jury.

[The Judge here suggested that the argument should be confined to the legal questions, and the argument on the other question suspended, until his opinion on those questions should be made known. This suggestion was assented to, and the counsel proceeded.]

My first position is that the defendant had the same right to vote as any other citizen who voted at that election.

Before proceeding to the discussion of the purely legal question, I desire, as already intimated, to pay some attention to the propriety and justice of the rule which I claim to have been established by the Constitution.

Miss Anthony, and those united with her in demanding the right of suffrage, claim, and with a strong appearance of justice, that upon the principles upon which our government is founded, and which lie at the basis of all just government, every citizen has a right to take part, upon equal terms with every other citizen, in the formation and administration of government. This claim on the part of the female sex presents a question the magnitude of which is not well appreciated by the writers and speakers who treat it with ridicule. Those engaged in the movement are able, sincere and earnest women, and they will not be silenced by such ridicule, nor even by the villainous caricatures of Nast. On the contrary, they justly place all those things to the account of the wrongs which they think their sex has suffered. They believe, with an intensity of feeling which men who have not associated with them have not yet learned, that their sex has not had, and has not now, its just and true position in the organization of government and society. They may be wrong in their position, but they will not be content until their arguments are fairly, truthfully and candidly answered.

In the most celebrated document which has been put forth on this side of the Atlantic, our ancestors declared that "governments derive their just powers from the consent of the governed."

Blackstone says, "The lawfulness of punishing such criminals (i. e., persons offending merely against the laws of society) is founded upon this principle: that the law by which they suffer was made by their own consent; it is a part of the original contract into which they entered when first they engaged in society; it was calculated for and has long contributed to their own security."

Quotations, to an unlimited extent, containing similar doctrines from eminent writers, both English and American, on government, from the time of John Locke to the present day, might be made. Without adopting this doctrine which bases the rightfulness of government upon the consent of the governed, I claim that there is implied in it the narrower and unassailable principle that all citizens of a State, who are bound by its laws, are entitled to an equal voice in the making and execution of such laws. The doctrine is well stated by Godwin in his treatise on Political Justice. He says: "The first and most important principle that can be imagined relative to the form and structure of government, seems to be this: that as government is a transaction in the name and for the benefit of the whole, every member of the community ought to have some share in its administration."

Again, "Government is a contrivance instituted for the security of individuals; and it seems both reasonable that each man should have a share in providing for his own security, and probable, that partiality and cabal should by this means be most effectually excluded."

And again, "To give each man a voice in the public concerns comes nearest to that admirable idea of which we should never lose sight, the uncontrolled exercise of private judgment. Each man would thus be inspired with a consciousness of his own importance, and the slavish feelings that shrink up the soul in the presence of an imagined superior would be unknown."

The mastery which this doctrine, whether right or wrong, has acquired over the public mind, has produced as its natural fruit, the extension of the right of suffrage to all the adult male population in nearly all the states of the Union; a result which was well epitomized by President Lincoln, in the expression, "government by the people for the people."

This extension of the suffrage is regarded by many as a source of danger to the stability of free government. I believe it furnishes the greatest security for free government, as it deprives the mass of the people of all motive for revolution; and that government so based is most safe, not because the whole people are less liable to make mistakes in government than a selet few, but because they have no interest which can lead them to such mistakes, or to prevent their correction when made. On the contrary, the world has never seen an aristocracy, whether composed of few or many, powerful enough to control a government, who did not honestly believe that their interest was identical with the public interest, and who did not act persistenly in accordance with such belief; and, unfortunately, an aristocracy of sex has not proved an exception to the rule. The only method yet discovered of overcoming this tendency to the selfish use of power, whether consciously or unconsciously, by those possessing it, is the distribution of the power among all who are its subjects. Short of this the name free government is a misnomer.

This principle, after long strife, not yet entirely ended has been, practically at least, very generally recognized on this side of the Atlantic, as far as relates to men; but when the attempt is made to extend it to women, political philosophers and practical politicians, those "inside of politics," two classes not often found acting in concert, join in denouncing it. It remains to be determined whether the reasons which have produced the extension of the franchise to all adult men, do not equally demand its extension to all adult women. If it be necessary for men that each should have a share in the administration of government for his security, and to exclude partiality, as alleged by Godwin, it would seem to be equally, if not more, necessary for women, on account of their inferior physical power: and if, as is persistently alleged by those who sneer at their claims, they are also inferior in mental power, that fact only gives additional weight to the argument in their behalf, as one of the primary objects of government, as acknowledged on all hands, is the protection of the weak against the power of the strong.

I can discover no ground consistent with the principle on which the franchise has been given to all men, upon which it can be denied to women. The principal argument against such extension, so far as argument upon that side of the question has fallen under my observation, is based upon the position that women are represented in the government by men, and that their rights and interests are better protected through that indirect representation than they would be by giving them a direct voice in the government.

The teachings of history in regard to the condition of women under the care of these self-constituted protectors, to which I can only briefly allude, show the value of this argument as applied to past ages; and in demonstration of its value as applied to more recent times, even at the risk of being tedious, I will give some examples from my own professional experience. I do this because nothing adds more to the efficacy of truth than the translation of the abstract into the concrete. Withholding names, I will state the facts with fullness and accuracy.

An educated and refined woman, who had been many years before deserted by her drunken husband, was living in a small village of Western New York, securing, by great economy and intense labor in fine needle work, the means of living, and of supporting her two daughters at an academy, the object of her life being to give them such an education as would enable them to become teachers, and thus secure to them some degree of independence when she could no longer provide for them. The daughters were good scholars, and favorites in the school, so long as the mother was able to maintain them there. A young man, the nephew and clerk of a wealthy but miserly merchant, became acquainted with the daughters, and was specially attentive to the older one. The uncle disapproved of the conduct of his nephew, and failing to control it by honorable means, resorted to the circulation of the vilest slanders against mother and daughters. He was a man of wealth and influence. They were almost unknown. The mother had but recently come to the village, her object having been to secure to her daughters the educational advantages which the academy afforded. Poverty, as well as perhaps an excusable if not laudable pride, compelled her to live in obscurity, and consequently the assault upon their characters fell upon her and her daughters with crushing force. Her employment mainly ceased, her daughters were of necessity withdrawn from school, and all were deprived of the means, from their own exertions, of sustaining life. Had they been in fact the harlots which the miserly scoundrel represented them to be, they would not have been so utterly powerless to resist his assault. The mother in her despair naturally sought legal redress. But how was it to be obtained? By the law the wife's rights were merged in those of the husband. She had in law no individual existence, and consequently no action could be brought by her to redress the grievous wrong; indeed *according to the law she had suffered no wrong*, but the husband had suffered all, and was entitled to all the redress. Where he was the lady did not know; she had not heard from him for many years. Her counsel, however, ventured to bring an action in her behalf, joining the husband's name with hers, as the law required. When the cause came to trial the defendant made no attempt to sustain the charges which he had made, well knowing that they were as groundless as they were cruel; but he introduced and proved a release of the cause of action, signed by the husband, reciting a consideration of fifty dollars paid to him. The defendant's counsel had some difficulty in proving the execution of the release, and was compelled to introduce as a witness, the constable who had been employed to find the vagabond husband and obtain his signature. His testimony disclosed the facts that he found the husband in the forest in one of our north-eastern counties, engaged in making shingles, (presumably stealing timber from the public lands and converting it into the means of indulging his habits of drunkenness,) and only five dollars of the fifty mentioned in the release had in fact been paid. The Court held, was compelled to hold, that the party injured *in view of the law*, had received full compensation for the wrong—and the mother and daughters with no means of redress were left to starve. This was the act of the *representative* of the wife and daughters to whom we are referred, as a better protector of their rights than they themselves could be.

It may properly be added, that if the action had proceeded to judgment without interference from the husband, and such amount of damages had been recovered as a jury might have thought it proper to award, the money would have belonged to the husband, and the wife could not lawfully have touched a cent of it. Her attorney might, and doubtless would have paid it to her, but he could only have done so at the peril of being compelled to pay it again to the drunken husband if he had demanded it.

In another case, two ladies, mother and daughter, some time prior to 1860 came from an eastern county of New York to Rochester, where a habeas corpus was obtained for a child of the daughter, less than two years of age. It appeared on the return of the writ, that the mother of the child had been previously abandoned by her husband, who had gone to a western state to reside, and his wife had returned with the child to her mother's house, and had resided there after her desertion. The husband had recently returned from the west, had succeeded in getting the child into his custody, and was stopping over night with it in Rochester on the way to his western home. No misconduct on the part of the wife was pretended, and none on the part of the husband, excepting that he had gone to the west leaving his wife and child behind, no cause appearing, and had returned, and somewhat clandestinely obtained posession of the child. The Judge, following Blackstone's views of husband's rights, remanded the infant to the custody of the father. He thought the law required it, and perhaps it did ; but if mothers had had a voice, either in making or in administering the law, I think the result would have been different. The distress of the mother on being thus separated from her child can be better imagined than described. The separation proved a final one, as in less than a year neither father nor mother had any child on earth to love or care for. Whether the loss to the little one of a mother's love and watchfulness had any effect upon the result, cannot, of course, be known.

The state of the law a short time since, in other respects, in regard to the rights of married women, shows what kind of security had been provided for them by their assumed representatives. Prior to 1848, all the personal property of every woman on marriage became the absolute property of the husband—the use of all her real estate became his during coverture, and on the birth of a living child, it became his during his life. He could squander it in dissipation or bestow it upon harlots, and the wife could not touch or interfere with it. Prior to 1860, the husband could by will take the custody of his infant children away from the surviving mother, and give it to whom he pleased—and he could in like manner dispose of the control of the children's property, after his death, during their minority, without the mother's consent.

In most of these respects the state of the law has undergone great changes within the last 25 years. The property, real and personal, which a woman possesses before marriage, and such as may be given to her during coverture, remains her own, and is free from the control of her husband.

If a married woman is slandered she can prosecute in her own name the slanderer, and recover to her own use damages for the injury.

The mother now has an equal claim with the father to the custody of their minor children, and in case of controversy on the subject, courts may award the custody to either in their discretion.

The husband cannot now by will effectually appoint a guardian for his infant children without the consent of the mother, if living.

These are certainly great ameliorations of the law; but how have they been produced? Mainly as the result of the exertions of a few heroic women, one of the foremost of whom is her who stands arraigned as a criminal before this Court to-day. For a thousand years the absurdities and cruelties to which I have alluded have been embedded in the common law, and in the statute books, and men have not touched them, and would not until the end of time, had they not been goaded to it by the persistent efforts of the noble women to whom I have alluded.

Much has been done, but much more remains to be done by women. If they had possessed the elective franchise, the reforms which have cost them a quarter of a century of labor would have been accomplished in a year. They are still subject to taxation upon their property, without any voice as to the levying or destination of the tax; and are still subject to laws *made by men*, which subject them to fine and imprisonment for the same acts which men do with honor and reward—and when brought to trial no woman is allowed a place on the bench or in the jury box, or a voice in her behalf at the bar. They are bound to suffer the penalty of such laws, made and administered solely by men, and to be silent under the infliction. Give them the ballot, and, although I do not suppose that any great revolution will be produced, or that all political evils will be removed, (I am not a believer in political panaceas,) but if I mistake not, valuable reforms will be introduced which are not now thought of. Schools, almshouses, hospitals, drinking saloons, and those worse dens which are destroying the morals and the constitutions of so many of the young of both sexes, will feel their influence to an extent now little dreamed of. At all events women will not be taxed without an opportunity to be heard, and will not be subject to fine and imprisonment by laws made exclusively by men for doing what it is lawful and honorable for men to do.

It may be said in answer to the argument in favor of female suffrage derived from the cases to which I have referred, that men, not individually, but collectively, are the natural and appropriate representatives of women, and that, notwithstanding cases of individual wrong, the rights of women are, on the whole, best protected by being left to their care. It must be observed, however, that the cases which I have stated, and which are only types of thousands like them, in their cruelty and injustice, are the result of ages of legislation by these assumed protectors of women. The wrongs were less in the men than in the laws which sustained them, and which contained nothing for the protection of the women.

But passing this view, let us look at the matter historically and on a broader field.

If Chinese women were allowed an equal share with men in shaping the laws of that great empire, would they subject their female children to torture with bandaged feet, through the whole period of childhood and growth, in order that they might be cripples for the residue of their lives?

If Hindoo women could have shaped the laws of India, would widows for ages have been burned on the funeral pyres of their deceased husbands?

If Jewish women had had a voice in framing Jewish laws, would the husband, at his own pleasure, have been allowed to "write his wife a bill of divorcement and give it in her hand, and send her out of his house"?

Would women in Turkey or Persia have made it a heinous, if not capital, offence for a wife to be seen abroad with her face not covered by an impenetrable veil?

Would women in England, however learned, have been for ages subjected to execution for offences for which men, who could read, were only subjected to burning in the hand and a few months imprisonment?

The principle which governs in these cases, or which has done so hitherto, has been at all times and everywhere the same. Those who succeed in obtaining power, no matter by what means, will, with rare exceptions, use it for their exclusive benefit. Often, perhaps generally, this is done in the honest belief that such use is for the best good of all who are affected by it. A wrong, however, to those upon whom it is inflicted, is none the less a wrong by reason of the good motives of the party by whom it is inflicted.

The condition of subjection in which women have been held is the result of this principle; the result of superior strength, not of superior rights, on the part of men. Superior strength, combined with ignorance and selfishness, but not with malice. It is a relic of the barbarism in the shadow of which nations have grown up. Precisely as nations have receded from barbarism the severity of that subjection has been relaxed. So long as merely physical power governed in the affairs of the world, the wrongs done to women were without the possibility of redress or relief; but since nations have come to be governed by laws, there is room to hope, though the process may still be a slow one, that injustice in all its forms, or at least politcal injustice, may be extingnished. No injustice can be greater than to deny to any class of citizens not guilty of crime, all share in the political power of a state, that is, all share in the choice of rulers, and in the making and administration of the laws. Persons to which such share is denied, are essentially slaves, because they hold their rights, if they can be said to have any, subject to the will of those who hold the political power. For this reason it has been found neccssary to give the ballot to the emancipated slaves. Until this was done their emancipation was far from complete. Without a share in the political powers of the state, no class of citizens has any security for its rights, and the history of nations to which I briefly alluded, shows that women constitute no exception to the universality of this rule.

Great errors, I think, exist in the minds of both the advocates and the opponents of this measure in their anticipation of the immediate effects to be produced by its adoption. On the one hand it is supposed by some that the character of women would be radically changed —that they would be unsexed, as it were, by clothing them with political rights, and that instead of modest, amiable and graceful beings, we should have bold, noisy and disgusting political demagogues, or something worse, if anything worse can be imagined. I think those who entertain such opinions are in error. The innate character of women is the result of God's laws, not of man's, nor can the laws of man affect that character beyond a very slight degree. Whatever rights may be given to them, and whatever duties may be charged upon them by human laws, their general character will remain unchanged. Their modesty, their delicacy, and intuitive sense of propriety, will never desert them, into whatever new positions their added rights or duties may carry them.

So far as women, without change of character as women, are qualified to discharge the duties of citizenship, they will discharge them if called upon to do so, and beyond that they will not go. Nature has put barriers in the way of any excessive devotion of women to public affairs, and it is not necessary that nature's work in that respect should be supplemented by additional barriers invented by men. Such offices as women are quaiified to fill will be sought by those who do not find other employment, and others they will not seek, or if they do, will seek in vain. To aid in removing as far as possible the disheartening difficulties which women dependent upon their own exertions encounter, it is, I think, desirable that such official positions as they can fill should be thrown open to them, and that they should be given the same power that men have to aid each other by their votes. I would say, remove all legal barriers that stand in the way of their finding employment, official or unofficial, and leave them as men are left, to depend for success upon their character and their abilities. As long as men are allowed to act as milliners, with what propriety can they exclude women from the post of school commissioners when chosen to such positions by their neighbors? To deny them such rights, is to leave them in a condition of political servitude as absolute as that of the African slaves before their emancipation. This conclusion is readily to be deduced from the opinion of Chief Justice Jay in the case of *Chisholm's Ex'rs vs. The State of Georgia* (*2 Dallas, 419-471*), although the learned Chief Justice had of course no idea of any such application as I make of his opinion.

The action was assumpsit by a citizen of the State of South Carolina, and the question was, whether the United States Court had jurisdiction, the State of Georgia declining to appear.

The Chief Justice, in the course of his opinion, after alluding to the feudal idea of the character of the sovereign in England, and giving some of the reasons why he was not subject to suit before the courts of the kingdom, says:

"The same feudal ideas run through all their jurisprudence, and constantly remind us of the distinction between the prince and the subject. No such ideas obtain here. At the revolution the sovereignty devolved on the people; and they are truly the sovereigns of the country, but *they are sovereigns without subjects* (unless the African slaves among us may be so called), and have none to govern but themselves; the citizens of America *are equal as fellow-citizens, and as joint tenants in the sovereignty.*"

Now I beg leave to ask, in case this charge against Miss Anthony can be sustained, what equality and what sovereignty is enjoyed by the half of the citizens of these United States to which she belongs? Do they not, in that event, occupy, *politically*, exactly the position which the learned Chief Justice assigns to the

African slaves? Are they not shown to be *subjects* of the other half, who are the sovereigns? And is not their *political subjection* as absolute as was that of the African slaves? If that charge has any basis to rest upon, the learned Chief Justice was wrong. The sovereigns of this country, according to the theory of this prosecution, are not sovereigns without subjects. Though two or three millions of their subjects have lately ceased to be such, and have become freemen, they still hold twenty millions of subjects in absolute *political* bondage.

If it be said that my language is stronger than the facts warrant, I appeal *to the record in this case* for its justification.

As deductions from what has been said, I respectfully insist, 1st, That upon the principles upon which our government is based, the privilege of the elective franchise cannot justly be denied to women. 2d. That women need it for their protection. 3d. That the welfare of both sexes will be promoted by granting it to them.

Having occupied much more time than I intended in showing the justice and propriety of the claim made by my client to the privileges of a voter, I proceed to the consideration of the present state of the law on that subject:

It would not become me, however clear my own convictions may be on the subject, to assert the right of women, under our constitution and laws as they now are, to vote at presidential and congressional elections, is free from doubt, because very able men have expressed contrary opinions on that question, and, so far as I am informed, there has been no authoritative adjudication upon it; or, at all events, none upon which the public mind has been content to rest as conclusive. I proceed, therefore, to offer such suggestions as occur to me, and to refer to such authorities bearing upon the question, as have fallen under my observation, hoping to satisfy your honor, not only that my client has committed no criminal offense, but that she has done nothing which she had not a legal and constitutional right to do.

It is not claimed that, under our State constitution and the laws made in pursuance of it, women are authorized to vote at elections, other than those of private corporations, and, consequently, the right of Miss Anthony to vote at the election in question, can only be established by reference to an authority superior to and sufficient to overcome the provisions of our State constitution. Such authority can only be found, and I claim that it is found in the constitution of the United States. For convenience I beg leave to bring together the various provisions of that constitution which bear more or less directly upon the question:

Article I, Section 2. "The House of Representatives shall be composed of members chosen every second year, by the people of the several States; and the electors in each State shall have the qualifications for electors of the most numerous branch of the State legislature."

The same Article, Section 3, "The Senate of the United States shall be composed of two senators from each State, chosen by the legislature thereof for six years; and each senator shall have one vote."

Article II, Section 1. "Each State shall appoint in such manner as the legislature thereof may direct, a number of electors equal to the whole number of senators and representatives to which the State may be entitled in the Congress."

Article IV, Section 2. "The citizens of each State shall be entitled to all the privileges and immunities of citizens in the several States."

Same Article, Section 4. "The United States shall guarantee to every State in the union a republican form of government."

THIRTEENTH AMENDMENT.

December 18, 1865.

"1. Neither slavery nor involuntary servitude, except as a punishment for crime, whereof the party shall have been duly convicted, shall exist within the United States, or any place subject to their jurisdiction."

"2. Congress shall have power to enforce this article by appropriate legislation."

FOURTEENTH AMENDMENT.

July 28, 1868.

Section 1. "All persons born or naturalized in the United States, and subject to the jurisdiction thereof, are citizens of the United States and of the State wherein they reside. No State shall make or enforce any law which shall abridge the privileges or immunities of citizens of the United States; nor shall any State deprive any person of life, liberty or property, without due process of law, nor deny to any person within its jurisdiction the equal protection of the laws."

Section 2. "Representatives shall be apportioned among the several States according to their respective numbers, counting the whole number of persons in each State, excluding Indians not taxed. But when the right to vote at any election for the choice of electors for President and Vice-President of the United States, Representatives in Congress, the Executive and Judicial officers of a State, or the members of the Legislature thereof, is denied to any of the male inhabitants of such State, being twenty-one years of age, and citizens of the United States, or in any way abridged, except for participation in rebellion or other crime, the basis of representation therein shall be reduced in the proportion which the number of such male citizens shall bear to the whole number of male citizens twenty-one years of age in such State."

* * * * * * *

Section 5. "The Congress shall have power to enforce, by appropriate legislation, the provisions of this article."

FIFTEENTH AMENDMENT.

Section 1. "The right of citizens of the United States to vote shall not be denied or abridged by the United States, or by any State, on account of race, color or previous condition of servitude."

Section 2. "The Congress shall have power to enforce this article by appropriate legislation."

By reference to the provisions of the original Constitution, here recited, it appears that prior to the thirteenth, if not until the fourteenth, amendment, the whole power over the elective franchise, even in the choice of Federal officers, rested with the States. The Constitution contains no definition of the term "citizen," either of the United States, or of the several States, but contents itself with the provision that "the citizens of each State shall be entitled to all the privileges and immunities of citizens of the several States." The States were thus left free to place such restrictions and limitations upon the "privileges and immunities" of citizens as they saw fit, so far as is consistent with a republican form of government, subject only to the condition that no State could place restrictions upon the "privileges or immunities" of the citizens of any other State, which would not be applicable to its own citizens under like circumstances.

It will be seen, therefore, that the whole subject, as to what should constitute the "privileges and immunities" of the citizen being left to the States, no question, such as we now present, could have arisen under the original constitution of the United States.

But now, by the fourteenth amendment, the United States have not only declared what constitutes citizenship, both in the United States and in the several States, securing the rights of citizens to "all persons born or naturalized in the United States;" but have absolutely prohibited the States from making or enforcing "*any law which shall abridge the privileges or immunities of citizens of the United States.*"

By virtue of this provision, I insist that the act of Miss Anthony in voting was lawful.

It has never, since the adoption of the fourteenth amendment, been questioned, and cannot be questioned, that women as well as men are included in the terms of its first section, nor that the same "privil ges and immunities of citizens" are equally secured to both.

What, then, are the "privileges and immunities of citizens of the United States" which are secured against such abridgement, by this section? I claim that these terms not only include the right of voting for public officers, but that they include that right as pre-eminently the most important of all the privileges and immunities to which the section refers. Among these privileges and immunities may doubtless be classed the right to life and liberty, to the acquisition and enjoyment of property, and to the free pursuit of one's own welfare, so far as such pursuit does not interfere with the rights and welfare of others; but what security has any one for the enjoyment of these rights when denied any voice in the making of the laws, or in the choice of those who make, and those who administer them? The possession of this voice, in the making and administration of the laws—this *political* right—is what gives security and value to the other rights, which are merely personal, not political. A person deprived of political rights is essentially a slave, because he holds his personal rights subject to the will of those who possess the political power. This principle constitutes the very corner-stone of our government—indeed, of all republican government. Upon that basis our separation from Great Britian was justified. "Taxation without representation is tyranny." This famous aphorism of James Otis, although sufficient for the occasion when it was put forth, expresses but a fragment of the principle, because government can be oppressive through means of many appliances besides that of taxation. The true principle is, that all government over persons deprived of any voice in such government, is tyranny. That is the principle of the declaration of independence. We were slow in allowing its application to the African race, and have been still slower in allowing its application to women; but it has been done by the fourteenth amendment, rightly construed, by a definition of "citizenship," which includes women as well as men, and in the declaration that "the privileges and immunities of citizens shall not be abridged." If there is any privilege of the citizen which is paramount to all others, it is the right of suffrage; and in a constitutional provision, designed to secure the most valuable rights of the citizen, the declaration that the privileges and immunities of the citizen shall not be abridged, must, as I conceive, be held to secure that right before all others. It is obvious, when the entire language of the section is examined, not only that this declaration was designed to secure to the citizen this *political* right, but that such was its principal, if not its sole object, those provisions of the section which follow it being devoted to securing the *personal* rights of "life, liberty, property, and the equal protection of the laws." The clause on which we rely, to wit:— "No State shall make or enforce any law which shall abridge the privileges or immunities of citizens of the United States," might be stricken out of the section, and the residue would secure to the citizen every right which is now secured, excepting the political rights of voting and holding office. *If the clause in question does not secure those political rights, it is entirely nugatory, and might as well have been omitted.*

If we go to the lexicographers and to the writers upon law, to learn what are the privileges and immunities of the "citizen" in a republican government, we shall find that the leading feature of citizenship is the enjoyment of the right of suffrage.

The definition of the term "citizen" by *Bouvier* is: "One who under the constitution and laws of the United States, has a right to vote for Representatives in Congress, and other public officers, and who is qualified to fill offices in the gift of the people."

By *Worcester*—"An inhabitant of a republic who enjoys the rights of a freeman, and has a right to vote for public officers."

By *Webster*—"In the United States, a person, native or naturalized, who has the privilege of exercising the elective franchise, or the qualifications which enable him to vote for rulers, and to purchase and hold real estate."

The meaning of the word "citizen" is directly and plainly recognized by the latest amendment of the constitution (the fifteenth.)

"*The right of the citizens of the United States to vote* shall not be denied or abridged by the United States, or by any State, on account of race, color, or previous condition of servitude." This clause assumes that the right of citizens, *as such*, to vote, is an existing right.

Mr. Richard Grant White, in his late work on Words and their Uses, says of the word citizen: "A citizen is a person who has certain political rights, and the word is properly used only to imply or suggest the possession of these rights."

Mr. Justice Washington, in the case of *Corfield vs. Coryell* (*4 Wash. C. C. Rep. 380*), speaking of the "privileges and immunities" of the citizen, as mentioned in Sec. 2, Art. 4, of the constitution, after enumerating the personal rights mentioned above, and some others, as embraced by those terms, says, "to which may be added the elective franchise, as regulated and established by the laws or constitution of the State in which it is to be exercised." At that time the States had entire control of the subject, and could abridge this privilege of the citizen at its pleasure; but the judge recognizes the "elective franchise" as among the "privileges and immunities" secured, to a qualified extent, to the citizens of every State by the provisions of the constitution last referred to. When, therefore, the States were, by the fourteenth amendment, absolutely prohibited from abridging the privileges of the citizen, either by enforcing existing laws, or by the making of new laws, the right of every "citizen" to the full exercise of this privilege, as against State action, was absolutely secured.

Chancellor Kent and Judge Story both refer to the opinion of Mr. Justice Washington, above quoted, with approbation.

The Supreme Court of Kentucky, in the case ot *Amy, a woman of color, vs. Smith* (*1 Littell's Rep. 326*), discussed with great ability the questions as to what constituted citizenship, and what were the "privileges and immunities of citizens" which were secured by Sec. 2, Art. 4, of the constitution, and they showed, by an unanswerable argument, that the term "citizens," as there used, was confined to those who were entitled to the enjoyment of the elective franchise, and that that was among the highest of the "privileges and immunities" secured to the citizen by that section. The court say that, "to be a citizen it is necessary that he should be entitled to the enjoyment of these privileges and immunities, upon the same terms upon which they are conferred upon other citizens; and unless he is so entitled, *he cannot, in the proper sense of the term, be a citizen.*"

In the case of *Scott vs. Sanford* (*19 How. 404,*) Chief Justice Taney says: "The words 'people of the United States,' and 'citizens,' are synonymous terms, and mean the same thing; they describe the *political body, who, according to our republican institutions, form the sovereignty and hold the power, and conduct the government through their representatives.* They are what we familiarly call the sovereign people, and every citizen is one of this people, and a constituent member of this sovereignty."

Mr. Justice Daniel, in the same case, (p. 476), says: "Upon the principles of etymology alone, the term citizen, as derived from *civitas,* conveys the idea of connection or identification with the state or government, and a participation in its functions. But beyond this, there is not, it is believed, to be found in the theories of writers on government, or in any actual experiment heretofore tried, an exposition of the term citizen, which has not been understood as conferring the actual possession and enjoyment, or the perfect right of acquisition and enjoyment of *an entire equality of privileges, civil and political.*"

Similar references might be made to an indefinite extent, but enough has been said to show that the term citizen, in the language of Mr. Justice Daniel, conveys the idea "of identification with the state or government, and a participation in its functions."

Beyond question, therefore, the first section of the fourteenth amendment, by placing the citizenship of women upon a par with that of men, and declaring that the "privileges and immunities" of the citizen shall not be abridged, has secured to women, equally with men, the right of suffrage, unless that conclusion is overthrown by some other provision of the constitution.

It is not necessary for the purposes of this argument to claim that this amendment prohibits a state from making or enforcing any law whatever, regulating the elective franchise, or prescribing the conditions upon which it may be exercised. But we do claim that in every republic the right of suffrage, in some form and to some extent, is not only one of the privileges of its citizens, but is the first, most obvious and most important of all the privileges they enjoy; that in this respect *all citizens are equal,* and that the effect of this amendment is, to prohibit the States from enforcing any law which denies this right to any of its citizens, or which imposes any restrictions upon it, which are inconsistent with a republican form of government. Within this limit, it is unnecessary for us to deny that the States may still regulate and control the exercise of the right.

The only provisions of the constitution, which it can be contended conflict with the construction which has here been put upon the first section of the fourteenth amendment, are the fifteenth amendment, and the second section of the fourteenth.

In regard to the fifteenth amendment, I shall only say, that if my interpretation of the fourteenth amendment is correct, there was still an object to be accomplished and which was accomplished by the fifteenth. The prohibition of any action abridging the privileges and immunities of citizens, contained in the fourteenth amendment, applies only to the States, and leaves the United States government free to abridge the political privileges and immunities of citizens of the United States, as such, at its pleasure. By the fifteenth amendment both the United States and the State governments, are prohibited from exercising this power, "on account of race, color, or previous condition of servitude" of the citizen.

The first remark to be made upon the second section of the fourteenth amendment is, that it does not give and was not designed to give to the States any power to deny or abridge the right of any citizen to exercise the elective franchise. So far as it touches that subject, it was designed to be restrictive upon the States. It gives to them no power whatever. It takes away no power, but it gives none, and if the States possess the power to deny or abridge the right of citizens to vote, it must be derived from some other provision of the constitution. I believe none such can be found, which was not necessarily abrogated by the first section of this amendment.

It may be conceded that the persons who prepared this section supposed, that, by other parts of the constitution, or in some other way, the States would still be authorized, notwithstanding the provisions of the first section, to deny to the citizens the privilege of voting, as mentioned in the second section; but their mistake cannot be held to add to, or to take from the other provisions of the constitution. It is very clear that they did not intend, by this section, *to give* to the States any such power, but, believieng that the States possessed it, they designed to hold the prospect of a reduction of their representation in Congress *in terrorem* over them to prevent them from exercising it. They seem not to have been able to emancipate themselves from the influence of the original constitution which conceded this power to the States, or to have realized the fact that the first section of the amendment, when adopted, would wholly deprive the States of that power.

But those who prepare constitutions are never those who adopt them, and consequently the views of those who frame them have little or no bearing upon their interpretation. The question for consideration here is, what the people, who, through their representatives in the legislatures, adopted the amendments, understood, or must be presumed to have understood, from their language. They must be presumed to have known that the "privileges and immunities" of citizens which were secured to them by the first section beyond the power of abridgment by the States, gave them the right to exercise the elective franchise, and they certainly cannot be presumed to have understood that the second section, which was also *designed to be restrictive* upon the States, would be held to confer by implication a power upon them, which the first section in the most express terms prohibited.

It has been, and may be again asserted, that the position which I have taken in regard to the second section is inadmissible, because it renders the section nugatory. That is, as I hold, an entire mistake. The leading object of the second section was the readjustment of the representation of the States in Congress, rendered necessary by the abolition of chattel slavery [*not of political slavery*], effected by the thirteenth amendment. This object the section accomplishes, and in this respect it remains wholly untouched, by my construction of it.

Neither do I think the position tenable which has been taken by one tribunal, to which the consideration of this subject was presented, that the constitutional provision does not execute itself.

The provisions on which we rely were negative merely, and were designed to nullify existing as well as any future State legislation interfering with our rights. This result was accomplished by the constitution itself. Undoubtedly before we could exercise our right, it was necessary that there should be a time and place appointed for holding the election and proper officers to hold it, with suitable arrangements for receiving and and counting the votes. All this was properly done by existing laws, and our right *being made complete by the Constitution, no further legislation was required in our behalf.* When the State officers attempted to interpose between us and the ballot-box the State Constitution or State law, whether ancient or recent, abridging or denying our equal right to vote with other citizens, we had but to refer to the United States Constitution, prohibiting the States from enforcing any such constitutional provision or law, and our rights were complete; we needed neither Congressional nor State legislation in aid of them.

The opinion of Mr. Justice Bradley, in a case in the United States Circuit Court in New Orleans (*1 Abb. U. S. Rep, 402*) would seem to be decisive of this question, although the right involved in that case was not that of the elective franchise. The learned justice says: "It was very ably contended on the part of the defendants that the fourteenth amendment was intended only to secure to all citizens *equal capacities before the law.* That was at first our view of it. But it does not so read. The language is: 'No State shall abridge the privileges or immunities of citizens of the United States.' What are the privileges and immunities of citizens? Are they capacities merely? Are they not also rights?"

Senator Carpenter, who took part in the discussion of the fourteenth amendment in the Senate, and aided in its passage, says: "The fourteenth amendment executes itself in every State of the Union. * * * * It is thus the will of the United States in every State, and silences every State Constitution, usage or law which conflicts with it. * * * * And if this provision does protect the colored citizen, then it protects every citizen, black or white, male or female. * * * And all the privileges and immunities which I vindicate to a colored citizen, I vindicate to our mothers, our sisters and our daughters."—*Chicago Legal News,* vol. iv., No. 15.

It has been said, with how much or how little truth I do not know, that the subject of securing to women the elective franchise was not considered in the preparation, or in the adoption of these amendments. It is wholly immaterial whether that was so or not. It is never possible to arrive at the intention of the people in adopting constitutions, except by referring to the language used. As is said by Mr. Cooley, "the intent is to be found in the instrument itself" (p. 55), and to that I have confined my remarks. It is not a new thing for constitutional and legislative acts to have an effect beyond the anticipation of those who framed them. It is undoubtedly true, that in exacting *Magna Charta* from King John, the Barons of England provided better securities for the rights of the common people than they were aware of at the time, although the rights of the common people were neither forgotten nor neglected by them. It has also been said, perhaps with some truth, that the framers of the original Constitution of the United States "builded better than they knew;" and it is quite possible that in framing the amendments under consideration, those engaged in doing it have accomplished a much greater work than they were at the time aware of. I am quite sure that it will be fortnnate for the country, if this great question of female suffrage, than which few greater were ever presented for the consideration of any people, shall be found, almost unexpectedly, to have been put at rest.

The opinion of Mr. Justice Bradley, in regard to this amendment, in the case before referred to, if I understand it, corresponds very nearly with what I have here said. The learned judge, in one part of his opinion, says: "It is possible that those who framed the article were not themselves aware of the far-reaching character of its terms. They may have had in mind but one particular phase of social and political wrong, which they desired to redress— yet, if the amendment, as framed and expressed, does, in fact, have a broader meaning, and does extend its protecting shield over those who were never thought of when it was conceived and put in form, and does reach such social evils which were never before prohibited by constitutional amendment, it is to be presumed that the American people, in giving it their imprimatur, understood what they were doing, and meant to decree what has, in fact, been done. * * * * * * *

"It embraces much more. The 'privileges and immunities' secured by the original Constitution were only such as each State gave its own citizens. Each was prohibited from discriminating in favor of its own citizens, and against the citizens of other States.

"But the fourteenth amendment prohibits any State from abridging the privileges or immunities of the citizens of the United States, whether its own citizens or any others. It not merely requires equality of privileges, but it demands that *the privileges and immunities of all citizens shall be absolutely unabridged, unimpaired.* (*1 Abbott's U. S. Rep. 397.*)

It will doubtless be urged as an objection to my position (that citizenship carries with it the right to vote) that it would, in that case, follow that infants and lunatics, who, as well as adults and persons of sound mind, are citizens, would also have that right. This objection, which appears to have great weight with certain classes of persons, is entirely without force. It takes no note of the familiar fact, that every legislative provision, whether constitutional or statutory, which confers any *discretionary* power, is always confined in its operation to persons who are *compos mentis.* It is wholly unnecessary to except idiots and lunatics out of any such statute. They are excluded from the very nature of the case. The contrary supposition would be simply absurd. And, in respect to every such law, infants, during their minority, are in the same class. But are women, *who are not infants,* ever included in this category? Does any such principle of exclusion apply to them? Not at all. On the contrary, they stand, in this respect, upon the same footing as men, with the sole exception of the right to vote and the right to hold office. In every other respect, whatever rights and powers are conferred upon persons by law may be exercised by women as well as by men. They may transact any kind of business for themselves, or as agents or trustees for others; may be executors or administrators, with the same powers and responsibilities as men; and it ought not to be a matter of surprise or regret that they are now placed, by the fourteenth amendment, in other respects upon a footing of perfect equality.

Although not directly connected with the argument as to the right secured to women by the Constitution, I deem it not improper to allude briefly to some of the popular objections against the propriety of allowing females the privilege of voting. I do this because I know from past experience that these popular objections, having no logical bearing upon the subject, are yet, practically, among the most potent arguments against the interpretation of the fourteenth amendment, which I consider the only one that its language fairly admits of.

It is said that woment do not desire to vote. Certainly many women do not, but that furnishes no reason for denying the right to those who do desire to vote. Many men decline to vote. Is that a reason for denying the right to those who would vote?

I believe, however, that the public mind is greatly in error in regard to the proportion of female citizens who would vote if their right to do so were recognized. In England there has been to some extent a test of that question, with the following result, as given in the newspapers, the correctness of which, in this respect, I think there is no reason to doubt:

"Woman suffrage is, to a certain extent, established in England, with the result as detailed in the London *Examiner*, that in 66 municipal elections, out of every 1,000 women who enjoy equal rights with men on the register, 516 went to the poll, which is but 48 less than the proportionate number of men. And out of 27,949 women registered, where a contest occurred, 14,416 voted. Of men there were 166,781 on the register, and 90,080 at the poll. The *Examiner* thereupon draws this conclusion: 'Making allowance for the reluctance of old spinsters to change their habits, and the more frequent illness of the sex, it is manifest that women, if they had opportunity, would exercise the franchise as freely as men. There is an end, therefore, of the argument that women would not vote if they had the power.'"

Our law books furnish, perhaps, more satisfactory evidence of the earnestness with which women in England are claiming the right to vote, under the reform act of 1867, aided by Lord Brougham's act of 1850.

The case of *Chorlton*, appellant, *vs. Lings*, respondent, came before the Court of Common Pleas in England in 1869. It was an appeal from the decision of the revising barrister, for the borough of Manchester, to the effect "that Mary Abbott, being a woman, was not entitled to be placed on the register." Her right was perfect in all respects excepting that of sex. The court, after a very full and able discussion of the subject, sustained the decision of the revising barrister, denying to women the right to be placed on the register, and consequently denying their right to vote. The decision rested upon the peculiar phraseology of several Acts of Parliament, and the point decided has no applicability here. My object in referring to the case has been to call attention to the fact stated by the reporter, *that appeals of 5,436 other women were consolidated and decided with this.* No better evidence could be furnished of the extent and earnestness of the claim of women in England to exercise the elective franchise.—*Law Rep. Com. Pleas, 4-374.*

I infer, without being able to say how the fact is, that the votes given by women, as mentioned in the newspapers, were given at municipal elections merely, and that the cases decided by the Court of Common Pleas relate to elections for members of Parliament.

Another objection is, that the right to hold office must attend the right to vote, and that women are not qualified to discharge the duties of responsible offices.

I beg leave to answer this objection by asking one or more questions. How many of the male bipeds who do our voting are qualified to hold high offices? How many of the large class to whom the right of voting is supposed to have been secured by the fifteenth amendment, are qualified to hold office?

Whenever the qualifications of persons to discharge the duties of responsible offices is made the test of their right to vote, and we are to have a competitive examination on that subject, open to all claimants, my client will be content to enter the lists, and take her chances among the candidates for such honors.

But the practice of the world, and our own practice, give the lie to this objection. Compare the administration of female sovereigns of great kingdoms, from Semiramis to Victoria, with the average administration of male sovereigns, and which will suffer by the comparison? How often have mothers governed large kingdoms, as regents, during the minority of their sons, and governed them well? Such offices as the "sovereigns" who rule them in this country have allowed women to hold (they having no voice on the subject), they have discharged the duties of with ever increasing satisfaction to the public; and Congress has lately passed an act, making the official bonds of married women valid, so that they could be appointed to the office of postmaster.

The case of *Olive vs. Ingraham* (*7 Modern Rep. 263*) was an action brought to try the title to an office. On the death of the sexton of the parish of St. Butolph, the place was to be filled by election, the voters being the housekeepers who "paid Scot and lot" in the parish. The widow of the deceased sexton (Sarah Bly) entered the lists against Olive, the plaintiff in the suit, and received 169 indisputable votes, and 40 votes given by women who were "housekeepers, and paid to church and poor." The plaintiff had 174 indisputable votes, and 22 votes given by such women as voted for Mrs. Bly. Mrs. Bly was declared elected. The action was brought to test two questions: 1. Whether women were legal voters; and 2. Whether a woman was capable of holding the office. The case was four times argued in the King's Bench, and all the judges delivered opinions, holding that the women were competent voters; that the widow was properly elected, and could hold the office.

In the course of the discussion it was shown that women had held many offices, those of constable, church warden, overseer of the poor, keeper of the "gate house" (a public prison), governess of a house of correction, keeper of castles, sheriffs of counties, and high constable of England.

If women are legally competent to hold minor offices, I would be glad to have the rule of law, or of propriety, shown which should exclude them from higher offices, and which marks the line between those which they may and those which they may not hold.

Another objection is that women cannot serve as soldiers. To this I answer that capacity for military service has never been made a test of the right to vote. If it were, young men from sixteen to twenty-one would be entitled to vote, and old men from sixty and upwards would not. If that were the test, some women would present much stronger claims than many of the male sex.

Another objection is that engaging in political controversies is not consistent with the feminine character. Upon that subject, women themselves are the best judges, and if political duties should be found inconsistent with female delicacy, we may rest assured that women will either effect a change in the character of political contests, or decline to engage in them. This subject may be safely left to their sense of delicacy and propriety.

If any difficulty on this account should occur, it may not be impossible to receive the votes of women at their places of residence. This method of voting was practiced in ancient Rome under the republic; and it will be remembered that when the votes of the soldiers who were fighting our battles in the Southern States were needed to sustain their friends at home, no difficulty was found in the way of taking their votes at their respective camps.

I humbly submit to your honor, therefore, that on the constitutional grounds to which I have referred, Miss Anthony had a lawful right to vote; that her vote was properly received and counted; that the first section of the fourteenth amendment secured to her that right, and did not need the aid of any further legislation.

But conceding that I may be in error in supposing that Miss Anthony had a right to vote, she has been guilty of no crime, if she voted in good faith believing that she had such right.

This proposition appears to me so obvious, that were it not for the severity to my client of the consequences which may follow a conviction, I should not deem it necessary to discuss it.

To make out the offence, it is incumbent on the prosecution to show affirmatively, not only that the defendant knowingly voted, but that she so voted *knowing that she had no right to vote.* That is, the term "knowingly," applies, not to the fact of voting, but to the fact of *want of right.* Any other interpretation of the language would be absurd. We cannot conceive of a case where a party could vote without knowledge of the fact of voting, and to apply the term "knowingly" to the mere act of voting, would make nonsense of the statute. This word was inserted as defining the essence of the offence, and it limits the criminality to cases where the voting is not only without right, but where it is done wilfully, with a *knowledge that it is without right.* Short of that there is no offence within the statute. This would be so upon well established principles, even if the word "knowingly" had been omitted, but that word was inserted to prevent the possibility of doubt on the subject, and to furnish security against the inability of stupid or prejudiced judges or jurors, to distinguish between wilful wrong and innocent mistake. If the statute had been merely, that "if at any election for representative in Congress any person shall vote without having a lawful right to vote, such person shall be deemed guilty of a crime," there could have been justly no conviction under it, without proof that the party voted *knowing* that he had not a right to vote. If he voted innocently supposing he had the right to vote, but had not, it would not be an offence within the statute. An innocent mistake is not a crime, and no amount of judicial decisions can make it such.

Mr. Bishop says, (1 Cr. Law, §205): "There can be no crime unless *a culpable intent* accompanies the criminal act." The same author, (1 Cr. Prac. §521), repeated in other words, the same idea: "In order to render a party criminally responsible, *a vicious will* must concur with a wrongful act."

I quote from a more distinguished author: "*Felony is always accompanied with an evil intention, and therefore shall not be imputed to a mere mistake, or misanimadversion*, as where persons break open a door, in order to execute a warrant, which will not justify such proceeding: *Affectio enim tua nomen imponit operi tuo: item crimen non contrahitur nisi nocendi, voluntas intercedat*," which, as I understand, may read: "For your volition puts the name upon your act; and *a crime is not committed unless the will of the offender takes part in it*."

1 Hawk. P. C., p. 99, Ch. 25, §3.

This quotation by Hawkins is, I believe, from Bracton, which carries the principle back to a very early period in the existence of the common law. It is a principle, however, which underlies all law, and must have been recognized at all times, wherever criminal law has been administered, with even the slightest reference to the principles of common morality and justice.

I quote again on this subject from Mr. Bishop: "The doctrine of *the intent* as it prevails in the criminal law, is necessarily *one of the foundation principles of public justicc*. There is only one criterion by which the guilt of man is to be tested. It is whether the mind is criminal. Criminal law relates only to crime. And neither in philosophical speculation, nor in religious or moral sentiment, would any people in any age allow that a man should be deemed guilty unless his mind was so. It is, therefore, a principle of our legal system, as probably it is of every other, that *the essence of an offence is the wrongful intent without which it cannot exist*." (*1 Bishop's Crim. Law, §287.*)

Again, the same author, writing on the subject of *knowledge*, as necessary to establish the intent, says: "It is absolutely necessary to constitute guilt, as in indictments for uttering forged tokens, or other attempts to defraud, or for receiving stolen goods, and offences of a similar description." (*1 Crim. Prac.* §504.)

In regard to the offence of obtaining property by false pretenses, the author says: "The indictment must allege that the defendant knew the pretenses to be false. *This is necessary upon the general principles of the law,* in order to show an offence, even though the statute does not contain the word "knowingly." (*2 Id.* §*172.*)

As to a *presumed knowledge* of the law, where the fact involves a question of law, the same author says: "The general doctrine laid down in the foregoing sections," (i. e. that every man is presumed to know the law, and that ignorance of the law does not excuse,) "is plain in itself aud plain in its application. Still there are cases, the precise nature and extent of which are not so obvious, wherein ignorance of the law constitutes, in a sort of indirect way, not in itself a defence, but a foundation on which another defence rests. Thus, if the guilt or innocence of a prisoner, depends on the fact to be found by the jury, of his having been or not, when he did the act, in some precise mental condition, *which mental condition is the gist of the offence,* the jury in determing this question of mental condition, *may* take into consideration his ignorance or misinformation in a matter of law. For example, to constitute larceny, there must be an intent to steal, which involves the knowledge that the property taken does not belong to the taker; yet, if all the facts concerning the title are known to the accused, and so the question is one merely of law whether the property is his or not, still he may show, and the showing *will be a defence* to him against the criminal proceeding, that he *honestly believed it his through a misapprehension of the law.*"

(1 Cr. Law, §297.)

The conclusions of the writer here, are correct, but in a part of the statement the learned author has thrown some obscurity over his own principles. The doctrines elsewhere enunciated by him, show with great clearness, that in such cases *the state of the mind constitutes the essence of the offence*, and if the state of the mind which the law condemns does not exist, in connection with the act, there is no offence. It is immaterial whether its non-existence be owing to ignorance of law or ignorance of fact, in either case the fact which the law condemns, the criminal intent, is wanting. It is not, therefore, in an "indirect way," that ignorance of the law in such cases constitutes a defence, but in the most direct way possible. It is not a fact which jurors "may take into consideration," or not, at their pleasure, but which they must take into consideration, because, in case the ignorance exists, no matter from what cause, *the offence which the statute describes is not committed.* In such case, ignorance of the law is not interposed as a shield to one committing a criminal act, but merely to show, as it does show, that no criminal act has been committed.

I quote from Sir Mathew Hale on the subject. Speaking of larceny, the learned author says: "As it is *cepit* and *asportavit*, so it must be *felonice*, or *animo furandi*, otherwise it is not felony, for *it is the mind* that makes the taking of another's goods to be a felony, or a bare trespass only ; but because the intention and mind are secret, the intention must be judged of by the circumstances of the fact, and these circumstances are various, and may sometimes deceive, yet regularly and ordinarily these circumstances following direct in the case. If A., thinking he hath a title to the house of B., seizeth it as his own * * this regularly makes no felony, but a trespass only ; but yet this may be a trick to colour a felony, and the ordinary discovery of a felonious intent is, if the party doth it secretly, or being charged with the goods denies it."

(1 Hales P. C. 509.)

I concede, that if Miss Anthony voted, knowing that as a woman she had no right to vote, she may properly be convicted, and that if she had dressed herself in men's apparel, and assumed a man's name, or resorted to any other artifice to deceive the board of inspectors, the jury might properly regard her claim of right, to be merely colorable, and might, in their judgment, pronounce her guilty of the offence charged, in case the constitution has not secured to her the right she claimed. All I claim is, that if she voted in perfect good faith, believing that it was her right, she has committed no crime. An innocent mistake, whether of law or fact, though a wrongful act may be done in pursuance of it, cannot constitute a crime.

[The following cases and authorities were referred to and commented upon by the counsel, as sustaining his positions: *U. S. vs. Conover, 3 McLean's Rep. 573* ; *The State vs. McDonald, 4 Harrington, 555* ; *The State vs. Homes, 17 Mo. 379* ; *Rex vs. Hall, 3 C. & P. 409, (S. C. 14 Eng. C. L.)*; *The Queen vs. Reed, 1 C. & M. 306. (S.*

C. 41 Eng. C. L.); Lancaster's Case, 3 Leon. 208; Starkie on Ev., Part IV, Vol. 2, p. 828, 3d Am. Ed.]

The counsel then said, there are some cases which I concede cannot be reconciled with the position which I have endeavoured to maintain, and I am sorry to say that one of them is found in the reports of this State. As the other cases are referred to in that, and the principle, if they can be said to stand on any principle, is in all of them the same, it will only be incumbent on me to notice that one. That case is not only irreconcilable with the numerous authorities and the fundamental principles of criminal law to which I have referred, but the enormity of its injustice is sufficient alone to condemn it. I refer to the case of *Hamilton vs. The People*, (*57 Barb. 725*). In that case Hamilton had been convicted of a misdemeanor, in having voted at a general election, after having been previously convicted of a felony and sentenced to two years imprisonment in the state prison, and not having been pardoned; the conviction having by law deprived him of citizenship and right to vote, unless pardoned and restored to citizenship. The case came up before the General Term of the Supreme Court, on writ of error. It appeared that on the trial evidence was offered, that before the prisoner was discharged from the state prison, he and his father applied to the Governor for a pardon, and that the Governor replied in writing, that on the ground of the prisoner's being a minor at the time of his discharge from prison, a pardon would not be necessary, and that he would be entitled to all the rights of a citizen on his coming of age. They also applied to two respectable counsellors of the Supreme Court, and they confirmed the Governor's opinion. All this evidence was rejected. It appeared that the prisoner was seventeen years old when convicted of the felony, and was nineteen when discharged from prison. The rejection of the evidence was approved by the Supreme Court on the ground that the prisoner was bound to know the law, and was presumed to do so, and his conviction was accordingly confirmed.

Here a young man, innocent so far as his conduct in this case was involved, was condemned, for acting in good faith upon the advice, (mistaken advice it may be conceded,) of one governor and two lawyers to whom he applied for information as to his rights; and this condemnation has proceeded upon the assumed ground, conceded to be false in fact, that he knew the advice given to him was wrong. On this judicial fiction the young man, in the name of justice, is sent to prison, punished for a mere mistake, and a mistake made in pursuance of such advice. It cannot be, consistently with the radical principles of criminal law to which I have referred, and the numerous authorities which I have quoted, that this man was guilty of a crime, that his *mistake* was a crime, and I think the judges who pronounced his condemnation, upon their own principles, better than their victim, deserved the punishment which they inflicted.

The condemnation of Miss Anthony, her good faith being conceded, would do no less violence to any fair administration of justice.

One other matter will close what I have to say. Miss Anthony believed, and was advised that she had a right to vote. She may also have been advised, as was clearly the fact, that the question as to her right could not be brought before the courts for trial, without her voting or offering to vote, and if either was criminal, the one was as much so as the other. Therefore she stands now arraigned as a criminal, for taking the only steps by which it was possible to bring the great constitutional question as to her right, before the tribunals of the country for adjudication. If for thus acting, in the most perfect good faith, with motives as pure and impulses as noble as any which can find place in your honor's breast in the administration of justice, she is by the laws of her country to be condemned as a criminal, she must abide the consequences. Her condemnation, however, under such circumstances, would only add another most weighty reason to those which I have already advanced, to show that women need the aid of the ballot for their protection.

Upon the remaining question, of the good faith of the defendant, it is not necessary for me to speak. That she acted in the most perfect good faith stands conceded.

Thanking your honor for the great patience with which you have listened to my too extended remarks, I submit the legal questions which the case involves for your honor's consideration.

THE COURT addressed the jury as follows:

Gentlemen of the Jury:

I have given this case such consideration as I have been able to, and, that there might be no no misapprehension about my views, I have made a brief statement in writing.

The defendant is indicted under the act of Congress of 1870, for having voted for Representatives in Congress in November, 1872. Among other things, that Act makes it an offence for any person knowingly to vote for such Representatives without having a right to vote. It is charged that the defendant thus voted, she not having a right to vote because she is a woman. The defendant insists that she has a right to vote ; that the provision of the Constitution of this State limiting the right to vote to persons of the male sex is in violation of the 14th Amendment of the Constitution of the United States, and is void. The 13th, 14th and 15th Amendments were designed mainly for the protection of the newly emancipated negroes, but full effect must nevertheless be given to the language employed. The 13th Amendment provided that neither slavery nor involuntary servitude should longer exist in the United States. If honestly received and fairly applied, this provision would have been enough to guard the rights of the colored race. In some States it was attempted to be evaded by enactments cruel and oppressive in their nature, as that colored persons were forbidden to appear in the towns except in a menial capacity ; that they should reside on and cultivate the soil without being allowed to own it ; that they were not permitted to give testimony in cases where a white man was a party. They were excluded from performing particular kinds of business, profitable and reputable, and they were denied the right of suffrage. To meet the difficulties arising from this state of things, the 14th and 15th Amendments were enacted.

The 14th Amendment created and defined citizenship of the United States. It had long been contended, and had been held by many learned authorities, and had never been judicially decided to the contrary, that there was no such thing as a citizen of the United States, except as that condition arose from citizenship of some State. No mode existed, it was said, of obtaining a citizenship of the United States except by first becoming a citizen of some State. This question is now at rest. The 14th Amendment defines and declares who should be citizens of the United States, to wit: "All persons born or naturalized in the United States and subject to the jurisdiction thereof." The latter qualification was intended to exclude the children of foreign representatives and the like. With this qualification every person born in the United States or naturalized is declared to be a citizen of the United States, and of the State wherein he resides. After creating and defining citizenship of the United States, the Amendment provides that no State shall make or enforce any law which shall abridge the privileges or immunities of a citizen of the United States. This clause is intended to be a protection, not to all our rights, but to our rights as citizens of the United States only; that is, the rights existing or belonging to that condition or capacity. The words "or citizen of a State," used in the previous paragraph are carefully omitted here. In article 4, paragraph 2, of the Constitution of the United States it had been already provided in this language, viz: "the citizens of each State shall be entitled to all the privileges and immunities of the citizens in the several States." The rights of citizens of the States and of citizens of the United States are each guarded by these different provisions. That these rights were separate and distinct, was held in the Slaughter House Cases recently decided by the United States Supreme Court at Washington. The rights of citizens of the State, as such, are not under consideration in the 14th Amendment. They stand as they did before the adoption of the 14th Amendment, and are fully guaranteed by other provisions. The rights of citizens of the States have been the subject of judicial decision on more than one occasion. *Corfield agt. Coryell, 4 Wash.; C. C. R., 371. Ward agt. Maryland; 12 Wall., 430. Paul agt. Virginia, 8 Wall., 140.*

These are the fundamental privileges and immunities belonging of right to the citizens of all free governments, such as the right of life and liberty; the right to acquire and possess property, to transact business, to pursue happiness in his own manner, subject to such restraint as the Government may adjudge to be necessary for the general good. In *Cromwell agt. Nevada, 6 Wallace, 36*, is found a statement of some of the rights of a citizen of the United States, viz: "To come to the seat of the Government to assert any claim he may have upon the Government, to transact any business he may have with it; to seek its protection; to share its offices; to engage in administering its functions. He has the right of free access to its seaports through which all operations of foreign commerce are conducted, to the sub-treasuries, land offices, and courts of justice in the several States." Another privilege of a citizen of the United States, says Miller, Justice, in the "Slaughter House" cases, is to demand the care and protection of the Federal Government over his life, liberty and property when on the high seas or within the jurisdiction of a foreign government. The right to assemble and petition for a redress of grievances, the privilege of the writ of *habeas corpus*, he says, are rights of the citizen guaranted by the Federal Constitution.

The right of voting, or the privilege of voting, is a right or privilege arising under the Constitution of the State, and not of the United States. The qualifications are different in the different States. Citizenship, age, sex, residence, are variously required in the different States, or may be so. If the right belongs to any particular person, it is because such person is entitled to it by the laws of the State where he offers to exercise it, and not because of citizenship of the United States. If the State of New York should provide that no person should vote until he had reached the age of 31 years, or after he had reached the age of 50, or that no person having gray hair, or who had not the use of all his limbs, should be entitled to vote, I do not see how it could be held to be a violation of any right derived or held under the Constitution of the United States. We might say that such regulations were unjust, tyrannical, unfit for the regulation of an intelligent State; but if rights of a citizen are thereby violated, they are of that fundamental class derived from his position as a citizen of the State, and not those limited rights belonging to him as a citizen of the United States, and such was the decision in *Corfield agt. Coryell.* (Supra.) The United States rights appertaining to this subject are those first under article 1, paragraph 2, of the United States Constitution, which provides that electors of Representatives in Congress shall have the qualifications requisite for electors of the most numerous branch of the State Legislature, and second, under the 15th Amendment, which provides that the right of a citizen of the United States to vote shall not be denied or abridged by the United States, or by any State, on account of race, color, or previous condition of servitude. If the Legislature of the State of New York should require a higher qualification in a voter for a representative in Congress than is required for a voter for a Member of Assembly, this would, I conceive, be a violation of a right belonging to one as a citizen of the United States. That right is in relation to a Federal subject or interest, and is guaranteed by the Federal Constitution. The inability of a State to abridge the right of voting on account of race, color, or previous condition of servitude, arises from a Federal guaranty. Its violation would be the denial of a Federal right—that is a right belonging to the claimant as a citizen of the United States.

This right, however, exists by virtue of the 15th Amendment. If the 15th Amendment had contained the word "sex," the argument of the defendant would have been potent. She would have said, an attempt by a State to deny the right to vote because one is of a particular sex, is expressly prohibited by that Amendment. The amendment, however, does not contain that word. It is limited to race, color, or previous condition of servitude. The Legislature of the State of New York has seen fit to say, that the franchise of voting shall be limited to the male sex. In saying this, there is, in my judgment, no violation of the letter or of the pirit of the 14th or of the 15th Amendment. This view is assumed in the second section of the 14th Amendment, which enacts that if the right to vote for Federal officers is denied by any state to any of the male inhabitants of such State, except for crime, the basis of representation of such State shall be reduced in proportion specified. Not only does this section assume that the right of male inhabitants to vote was the especial object of its protection, but it assumes and admits the right of a State, notwithstanding the existence of that clause under which the defendant claims to the contrary, to deny to classes or portions of the male inhabitants the right to vote which is allowed to other male inhabitants. The regulation of the suffrage is thereby conceded to the States as a State's right. The case of Myra Bradwell, decided at a recent term of the Supreme Court of the United States, sustains both the positions above put forth, viz: First, that the rights referred to in the 14th Amendment are those belonging to a person as a citizen of the United States and not as a citizen of a State, and second, that a right of the character here involved is not one connected with citizenship of the United States. Mrs. Bradwell made application to be admitted to practice as an attorney and counsellor at law, in the Courts of Illinois. Her application was denied, and upon appeal to the Supreme Court of the United States, it was there held that to give jurisdiction under the 14th Amendment, the claim must be of a right pertaining to citizenship of the United States, and that the claim made by her did not come within that class of cases. Mr. Justice Bradley and Mr. Justice Field held that a woman was not entitled to a license to practice law. It does not appear that the other Judges passed upon that question.

The 14th Amendment gives no right to a woman to vote, and the voting by Miss Anthony was in violation of the law.

If she believed she had a right to vote, and voted in reliance upon that belief, does that relieve her from the penalty? It is argued that the knowledge referred to in the act relates to her knowledge of the illegality of the act, and not to the act of voting; for it is said that she must know that she voted. Two principles apply here: First, ignorance of the law excuses no one; second, every person is presumed to understand and to intend the necessary effects of his own acts. Miss Anthony knew that she was a woman, and that the constitution of this State prohibits her from voting. She intended to violate that provision—intended to test it, perhaps, but certainly intended to violate it. The necessary effect of her act was to violate it, and this she is presumed to have intended. There was no ignorance of any fact, but all the facts being known, she undertook to settle a principle in her own person. She takes the risk, and she cannot escape the consequences. It is said, and authorities are cited to sustain the position, that there can be no crime unless there is a culpable intent; to render one criminally responsible a vicious will must be present. A commits a trespass on the land of B, and B, thinking and believing that he has a right to shoot an intruder on his premises, kills A on the spot. Does B's misapprehension of his rights justify his act? Would a Judge be justified in charging the jury that if satisfied that B supposed he had a right to shoot A he was justified, and they should find a verdict of not guilty? No Judge would make such a charge. To constitute a crime, it is true, that there must be a criminal intent, but it is equally true that knowledge of the facts of the case is always held to supply this intent. An intentional killing bears with it evidence of malice in law. Whoever, without justifiable cause, intentionally kills his neighbor, is guilty of a crime. The principle is the same in the case before us, and in all criminal cases. The precise question now before me has been several times decided, viz.: that one illegally voting was bound and was assumed to know the law, and that a belief that he had a right to vote gave no defense, if there was no mistake of fact. (Hamilton against The People, 57th of Barbour, p. 625; State against Boyet, 10th of Iredell, p. 336; State against Hart, 6th Jones, 389; McGuire against State, 7 Humphrey, 54; 15th of Iowa reports, 404.) No system of criminal jurisprudence can be sustained upon any other principle. Assuming that Miss Anthony believed she had a right to vote, that fact constitutes no defense if in truth she had not the right. She voluntarily gave a vote which was illegal, and thus is subject to the penalty of the law.

Upon this evidence I suppose there is no question for the jury and that the jury should be directed to find a verdict of guilty.

JUDGE SELDEN: I submit that on the view which your Honor has taken, that the right to vote and the regulation of it is solely a State matter. That this whole law is out of the jurisdiction of the United States Courts and of Congress. The whole law upon that basis, as I understand it, is not within the constitutional power of the general Government, but is one which applies to the States. I suppose that it is for the jury to determine whether the defendant is guilty of a crime or not. And I therefore ask your Honor to submit to the jury these propositions:

First—If the defendant, at the time of voting, believed that she had a right to vote and voted in good faith in that belief, she is not guilty of the offense charged.

Second—In determining the question whether she did or did not believe that she had a right to vote, the jury may take into consideration, as bearing upon that question, the advice which she received from the counsel to whom she applied.

Third—That they may also take into consideration, as bearing upon the same question, the fact that the inspectors considered the question and came to the conclusion that she had a right to vote.

Fourth—That the jury have a right to find a general verdict of guilty or not guilty as they shall believe that she has or has not committed the offense described in the Statute.

A professional friend sitting by has made this suggestion which I take leave to avail myself of as bearing upon this question: "The Court has listened for many hours to an argument in order to decide whether the defendant has a right to vote. The arguments show the same question has engaged the best minds of the country as an open question. Can it be possible that the defendant is to be convicted for acting upon such advice as she could obtain while the question is an open and undecided one?

THE COURT: You have made a much better argument than that, sir.

JUDGE SELDEN: As long as it is an open question I submit that she has not been guilty of an offense. At all events it is for the jury.

THE COURT: I cannot charge these propositions of course. The question, gentlemen of the jury, in the form it finally takes, is wholly a question or questions of law, and I have decided as a question of law, in the first place, that under the 14th Amendment, which Miss Anthony claims protects her, she was not protected in a right to vote. And I have decided also that her belief and the advice which she took does not protect her in the act which she committed. If I am right in this, the result must be a verdict on your part of guilty, and I therefore direct that you find a verdict of guilty.

JUDGE SELDEN: That is a direction no Court has power to make in a criminal case.

THE COURT: Take the verdict, Mr. Clerk.

THE CLERK: Gentlemen of the jury, hearken to your verdict as the Court has recorded it. You say you find the defendant guilty of the offense whereof she stands indicted, and so say you all?

JUDGE SELDEN: I don't know whether an exception is available, but I certainly must except to the refusal of the Court to submit those propositions, and especially to the direction of the Court that the jury should find a verdict of guilty. I claim that it is a power that is not given to any Court in a criminal case.

Will the Clerk poll the jury?

THE COURT; No. Gentlemen of the jury, you are discharged.

On the next day a motion for a new trial was made by Judge Selden, as follows:

May it please the Court:

The trial of this case commenced with a question of very great magnitude—whether by the constitution of the United States the right of suffrage was secured to female equally with male citizens. It is likely to close with a question of much greater magnitude—whether the right of trial by jury is absolutely secured by the federal constitution to persons charged with crime before the federal courts.

I assume, without attempting to produce any authority on the subject, that this Court has power to grant to the defendant a new trial in case it should appear that in the haste and in the lack of opportunity for examination which necessarily attend a jury trial, any material error should have been committed prejudicial to the defendant, as otherwise no means whatever are provided by the law for the correction of such errors.

The defendant was indicted, under the nineteenth section of the act of Congress of May 31st, 1870, entitled, "An act to enforce the right of citizens of the United States to vote in the several states of this Union, and for other purposes," and was charged with having knowingly voted, without having a lawful right to vote, at the congressional election in the eighth ward of the City of Rochester, in November last; the only ground of illegality being that the defendant was a woman.

The provisions of the act of Congress, so far as they bear upon the present case, are as follows:

"Section 19. If at any election for representative or delegate in the Congress of the United States, any person shall knowingly personate and vote, or attempt to vote, in the name of any other person, whether living, dead or fictitious, or vote more than once at the same election for any candidate for the same office, or vote at a place where he may not be lawfully entitled to vote, or vote without having a lawful right to vote, * * * every such person shall be deemed guilty of a crime, and shall for such crime be liable to prosecution in any court of the United States, of competent jurisdiction, and, on conviction thereof, shall be punished by a fine not exceeding $500 or by imprisonment for a term not exceeding three years, or both, in the discretion of the Court, and shall pay the costs of prosecution."

It appeared on the trial that before voting the defendant called upon a respectable lawyer, and asked his opinion whether she had a right to vote, and he advised her that she had such right, and the lawyer was examined as a witness in her behalf, and testified that he gave her such advice, and that he gave it in good faith, believing that she had such right.

It also appeared that when she offered to vote, the question whether as a woman she had a right to vote, was raised by the inspectors, and considered by them in her presence, and they decided that she had a right to vote, and received her vote accordingly.

It was also shown on the part of the government, that on the examination of the defendant before the commissioner, on whose warrant she was arrested, she stated that she should have voted, if allowed to vote, without reference to the advice she had received from the attorney whose opinion she had asked; that she was not influenced to vote by that opinion; that she had before determined to offer her vote, and had no doubt about her right to vote.

At the close of the testimony the defendant's counsel proceeded to address the jury, and stated that he desired to present for consideration three propositions, two of law and one of fact:

First—That the defendant had a lawful right to vote.

Second—That whether she had a lawful right to vote or not, it she honestly belleved that she had that right and voted in good faith in that belief, she was guilty of no crime.

Third—That when she gave her vote she gave it in good faith, believing that it was her right to do so.

That the two first propositions presented questions for the Court to decide, and the last for the jury.

When the counsel had proceeded thus far, the Court suggested that the counsel had better discuss in the first place the questions of law; which the counsel proceeded to do, and having discussed the two legal questions at length, asked leave then to say a few words to the jury on the question of fact. The Court then said to the counsel that he thought that had better be left until the views of the Court upon the legal questions should be made known.

The District Attorney thereupon addressed the Court at length upon the legal questions, and at the close of his argument the Court delivered an opinion adverse to the positions of the defendant's counsel upon both of the legal questions presented, holding that the defendant was not entitled to vote; and that if she voted in good faith in the belief in fact that she had a right to vote, it would constitute no defense—the grounds of the decision on the last point being that she was bound to know that by law she was not a legal voter, and that even if she voted in good faith in the contrary belief, it constituted no defense to the crime with which she was charged. The decision of the Court upon these questions was read from a written document.

At the close of the reading, the Court said that the decision of these questions disposed of the case and left no question of fact for the jury, and that he should therefore direct the jury to find a verdict of guilty, and proceeded to say to the jury that the decision of the Court had disposed of all there was in the case, and that he directed them to find a verdict of guilty, and he instructed the clerk to enter a verdict of guilty.

At this point, before any entry had been made by the clerk, the defendant's counsel asked the Court to submit the case to the jury, and to give to the jury the following several instructions:

First—That if the defendant, at the time of voting, believed that she had a right to vote, and voted in good faith in that belief, she is not guilty of the offence charged.

Second—In determining the question whether she did or did not believe that she had a right to vote, the jury may take into consideration, as bearing upon that question, the advice which she received from the counsel to whom she applied.

Third—That they may also take into consideration as bearing upon the same question, the fact that the inspectors considered the question, and came to the conclusion that she had a right to vote.

Fourth—That the jury have a right to find a general verdict of guilty or not guilty, as they shall believe that she has or has not been guilty of the offense described in the statute.

The Court declined to submit the case to the jury upon any question whatever, and directed them to render a verdict of guilty against the defendant.

The defendant's counsel excepted to the decision of the Court upon the legal questions to its refusal to submit the case to the jury; to its refusal to give the instructions asked; and to its direction to the jury to find a verdict of guilty against the defendant—the counsel insisting that it was a direction which no Court had a right to give in a criminal case.

The Court then instructed the clerk to take the verdict, and the clerk said, "Gentlemen of the jury, hearken to the verdict as the Court hath recorded it. You say you find the defendant guilty of the offence charged. So say you all."

No response whatever was made by the jury, either by word or sign. They had not consulted together in their seats or otherwise. Neither of them had spoken a word. Nor had they been asked whether they had or had not agreed upon a verdict.

The defendant's counsel then asked that the clerk be requested to poll the jury. The Court said, "that cannot be allowed. Gentlemen of the jury, you are discharged," and the jurors left the box. No juror spoke a word during the trial, from the time they were impanelled to the time of their discharge.

Now I respectfully submit, that in these proceedings the defendant has been substantially denied her constitutional right of trial by jury. The jurors composing the panel have been merely silent spectators of the conviction of the defendant by the Court. They have had no more share in her trial and conviction than any other twelve members of the jury summoned to attend this Court, or any twelve spectators who have sat by during the trial. If such course is allowable in this case, it must be equally allowable in all criminal cases, whether the charge be for treason, murder or any minor grade of offence which can come under the jurisdiction of a United States court; and as I understand it, if correct, substantially abolishes the right of trial by jury.

It certainly does so in all those cases, where the judge shall be of the opinion that the facts which he may regard as clearly proved, lead necessarily to the guilt of the defendant. Of course by refusing to submit any question to the jury, the judge refuses to allow counsel to address the jury in the defendant's behalf.

The constitutional provisions which I insist are violated by this proceeding are the following:

Constitution of the United States, article 3, section 2. "The trial of all crimes, except in cases of impeachment, shall be by jury."

Amendments to Constitution, article 6. "In all criminal prosecutions, the accused shall enjoy the right to a speedy and public trial, by an impartial jury of the State and District wherein the crime shall have been committed, which district shall have been previously ascertained by law; and to be informed of the nature and cause of the accusation ; to be confronted with the witnesses against him ; to have compulsory process for obtaining witnesses in his favor, and to have the assistance of counsel for his defense."

In accordance with these provisions, I insist that in every criminal case, where the party has pleaded not guilty, whether upon the trial the guilt of such party appears to the Judge to be clear or not, the response to the question, guilty or not guilty, must come from the jury, must be their voluntary act, and cannot be imposed upon them by the Court.

No opportunity has been given me to consult precedents on this subject, but a friend has referred me to an authority strongly supporting my position, from which I will quote, though I deem a reference to precedents unnecessary to sustain the plain declarations of the Constitution: I refer to the case of the *State vs. Shule*, (*10 Iredell, 153*,) the substance of which is stated in *2 Graham & Waterman* on New Trials, page 363. Before stating that case I quote from the text of G. & W.

"The verdict is to be the r-sult of the deliberation of the jury upon all the evidence in the case. The Court has no right to anticipate the verdict by an expression of opinion calculated so to influence the jury as to take from them their independence of action."

In the *State vs. Shule*, two defendants were indicted for an affray. "The jury remaining out a considerable time, at the request of the prosecuting attorney they were sent for by the Court. The Court then charged them that although Jones, (the other defendant,) had first commenced a battery upon Shule, yet, if the jury believed the evidence, the defendant, Shule, was also guilty. Thereupon, one of the jurors remarked that they had agreed to convict Jones, but were about to acquit Shule. The Court then charged the jury again, and told them that they could retire if they thought proper to do so. The jury consulted together a few minutes in the Court room. The prosecuting attorney directed the clerk to enter a verdict of guilty as to both defendants. When the clerk had entered the verdict, the jury were asked to attend to it, as it was about to be read by the clerk. The clerk then read the verdict in the hearing of the jury. The jury, upon being requested, if any of them disagreed to the verdict to make, it known by a nod, seemed to express their unanimous assent; and no juror expressed his dissent." In reviewing the case the Court say: "The error complained of is, that before the jury had announced their verdict, and in fact after they had intimated an intention to acquit the defendant, Shule, the Court allowed the clerk to be directed to enter a verdict finding him guilty, and after the verdict was so entered, allowed the jury to be asked if any of them disagreed to the verdict which had been recorded by the clerk. No juror expressed his dissent; but by a nod which appeared to be made by each juror, expressed their unanimous assent. The innovation is, that instead of permitting the jury to give their verdict, the Court allows a verdict to be entered for them, such as it is to be presumed the Court thinks they ought to render, and then they are asked if any of them disagree to it; thus making a verdict for them, unless they are bold enough to stand out against a plain intimation of the opinion of the Court." A *venire de novo* was ordered. The principal difference between this case and the one under consideration is, that in the latter the Court directed the clerk to enter the verdict, and in the former he was allowed to do so, and in the latter the Court denied liberty to the jurors to dissent from the verdict, and in the former the Court allowed such dissent.

With what jealous care the right of trial by jury in criminal cases has been guarded by every English speaking people from the days of King John, indeed from the days of King Alfred, is known to every lawyer and to every intelligent layman, and it does not seem to me that such a limitation of that right as is presented by the proceedings in this case, can be reconciled either with constitutional provisions, with the practice of courts, with public sentiment on the subject, or with safety in the administration of justice. How the question would be regarded by the highest Court of this State may fairly be gathered from its decision in the case of *Cancemi, 18 N. Y., 128*, where, on a trial for murder, one juror, some time after the trial commenced, being necessarily withdrawn, a stipulation was entered into, signed by the District-Attorney, and by the defendant and his counsel, to the effect that the trial should proceed before the remaining eleven jurors, and that their verdict should have the same effect as the verdict of a full panel would have. A verdict of guilty having been rendered by the eleven jurors, was set aside and a new trial ordered by the Court of Appeals, on the ground that the defendant could not, even by his own consent, be lawfully tried, by a less number of jurors than twelve. It would seem to follow that he could not waive the entire panel, and effectually consent to be tried by the Court alone, and still less could the Court, against his protest, assume the duties of the jury, and effectually pronounce the verdict of guilty or not guilty in their stead.

It will doubtless be insisted that there was no disputed question of fact upon which the jury were required to pass. In regard to that, I insist that however clear and conclusive the proof of the facts might appear to be, the response to the question, guilty or not guilty, must under the Constitution come from the jury and could not be supplied by the judgment of the Court, unless, indeed, the jury should see fit to render a special verdict, which they always may, but can never be required, to do.

It was the province of the Court to instruct the jury as to the law, and to point out to them how clearly the law, on its view of the established facts, made out the offence; but it has no authority to instruct them positively on any question of fact, or to order them to find any particular verdict. That must be their spontaneous work.

But there was a question of fact, which constituted the very essence of the offence, and one on which the jury were not only entitled to exercise, but were in duty bound to exercise, their independent judgment. That question of fact was, whether the defendant, at the time when she voted, knew that she had not a right to vote. The statute makes this knowledge the very gist of the offence, without the existence of which, in the mind of the voter, at the time of voting, there is no crime. There is none by the statute and none in morals. The existence of this knowledge, in the mind of the voter, at the time of voting, is under the statute, necessarily a fact and nothing but a fact, and one which the jury was bound to find as a fact, before they could, without violating the statute, find the defendant guilty. The ruling which took that question away from the jury, on the ground that it was a question of law and not of fact, and which declared that as a question of law, the knowledge existed, was, I respectfully submit, a most palpable error, both in law and justice. It was an error in law, because its effect was to deny any force whatever to the most important word which the statute uses in defining the offense—the word "knowingly." It was also unjust, because it makes the law declare a known falsehood as a truth, and then by force of that judicial falsehood condemns the defendant to such punishment as she could only lawfully be subject to, if the falsehood were a truth.

I admit that it is an established legal maxim that every person (judicial officers excepted) is bound, and must be presumed, to know the law. The soundness of this maxim, in all the cases to which it can properly be applied, I have no desire to question; but it has no applicability whatever to this case. It applies in every case where a party does an act which the law pronounces criminal, whether the party knows or does not know that the law has made the act a crime. That maxim would have applied to this case, if the defendant had voted, knowing that she had no legal right to vote; without knowing that the law had made the act of knowingly voting without a right, a crime. In that case she would have done the act which the law made a crime, and could not have shielded herself from the penalty by pleading ignorance of the law. But in the present case the defendant has not done the act which the law pronounces a crime. The law has not made the act of voting without a lawful right to vote, a crime, where it is done by mistake, and in the belief by the party voting that he has the lawful right to vote. The crime consists in voting "knowingly," without lawful right. Unless the knowledge exists in fact, is the very gist of the offence is wanting. To hold that the law presumes conclusively that such knowledge exists in all cases where the legal right is wanting, and to reject all evidence to the contrary, or to deny to such evidence any effect, as has been done on this trial, is to strike the word "knowingly" out of the statute—and to condemn the defendant on the legal fiction that she was acting in bad faith, it being all the while conceeded that she was in fact acting in good faith. I admit that there are precedents to sustain such ruling, but they cannot be reconciled with the fundamental principles of criminal law, nor with the most ordinary rules of justice. Such a ruling cannot but shock the moral sense of all right-minded, unprejudiced men.

No doubt the assumption by the defendant of a belief of her right to vote might be made use of by her as a mere cover to secure the privilege of giving a known illegal vote, and of course that false assumption would constitute no defence to the charge of illegal voting. If the defendant had dressed herself in male attire, and had voted as John Anthony, instead of

Susan, she would not be able to protect herself against a charge of voting with a knowledge that she had no right to vote, by asserting her belief that she had a right to vote as a woman. The artifice would no doubt effectually overthrow the assertion of good faith. No such question, however, is made here. The decision of which I complain concedes that the defendant voted in good faith, in the most implicit belief that she had a right to vote, and condemns her on the strength of the legal fiction, conceded to be in fact a mere fiction, that she knew the contrary.

But if the facts admitted of a doubt of the defendant's good faith, that was a question for the jury, and it was clear error for the court to assume the decision of it.

Again. The denial of the right to poll the jury was most clearly an error. Under the provisions of the constitution which have been cited, the defendant could only be convicted on the verdict of a jury. The case of Cancemi shows that such jury must consist of twelve men; and it will not be claimed that anything less than the unanimous voice of the jury can be received as their verdict. How then could the defendant be lawfully deprived of the right to ask every juror if the verdict had his assent? I believe this is a right which was never before denied to a party against whom a verdict was rendered in any case, either civil or criminal. The following cases show, and many others might be cited to the same effect, that the right to poll the jury is an absolute right in all cases, civil and criminal. (The People vs. Perkins, 1 Wend. 91. Jackson vs. Hawks, 2 Wend. 619. Fox vs. Smith, 3 Cowen, 23.)

The ground on which the right of the defendant to vote has been denied, is, as I understand the decision of the court, "that the rights of the citizens of the state as such were not under consideration in the fourteenth amendment; that they stand as they did before that amendment. * * * * * *

The right of voting or the privilege of voting is a right or privilege arising under the constitution of the state, and not of the United States. If the right belongs to any particular person, it is because such person is entitled to it as a citizen of the state where he offers to exercise it, and not because of citizenship of the United States. * * * The regulation of the suffrage is conceded to the states as a state right."

If this position be correct, which I am not now disposed to question, I respectfully insist that the congress of the United States had no power to pass the act in question, that by doing so it has attempted to usurp the rights of the states, and that all proceedings under the act are void.

I claim therefore that the defendant is entitled to a new trial.

First—Because she has been denied her right of trial by jury.

Second—Because she has been denied the right to ask the jury severally whether they assented to the verdict which the court had recorded for them.

Third—Because the court erroneously held, that the defendant had not a lawful right to vote.

Fourth—Because the court erroneously held, that if the defendant, when she voted, did so in good faith, believing that she had a right to vote, that fact constituted no defence.

Fifth.—Because the court erroneously held that the question, whether the defendant at the time of voting knew that she had not a right to vote, was a question of law to be decided by the court, and not a question of fact to be decided by the jury.

Sixth—Because the court erred in holding that it was a presumption of law that the defendant knew that she was not a legal voter, although in fact she had not that knowledge.

Seventh—Because congress had no constitutional right to pass the act under which the defendant was indicted, and the act and all proceedings under it are void.

Sir, so far as my information in regard to legal proceedings extends, this is the only court in any country where trial by jury exists, in which the decisions that are made in the haste and sometimes confusion of such trials, are not subject to review before any other tribunal. I believe that to the decisions of this court, in criminal cases, no review is allowed, except in the same court in the informal way in which I now ask your honor to review the decisions made on this trial. This is therefore the court of last resort, and I hope your honor will give to these, as they appear to me, grave questions, such careful and deliberate consideration as is due to them from such final tribunal.

If a new trial shall be denied to the defendant, it will be no consolation to her to be dismissed with a slight penalty, leaving the stigma resting upon her name, of conviction for an offence, of which she claims to be, and I believe is, as innocent as the purest of the millions of male voters who voted at the same election, are innocent of crime in so voting. If she is in fact guilty of the crime with which she stands charged, and of which she has been convicted by the court, she deserves the utmost penalty which the court under the law has power to impose; if she is not guilty she should be acquitted, and not declared upon the records of this high court guilty of a crime she never committed.

The court after hearing the district attorney, denied the motion.

Judge Hunt—(Ordering the defendant to stand up), "Has the prisoner anything to say why sentence shall not be pronounced?"

MISS ANTHONY—Yes, your honor, I have many things to say; for in your ordered verdict of guilty, you have trampled under foot every vital principle of our government. My natural rights, my civil rights, my political rights, my judicial rights, are all alike ignored. Robbed of the fundamental privilege of citizenship, I am degraded from the status of a citizen to that of a subject; and not only myself individually, but all of my sex, are, by your honor's verdict, doomed to political subjection under this, so-called, form of government.

JUDGE HUNT—The Court cannot listen to a rehearsal of arguments the prisoner's counsel has already consumed three hours in presenting.

MISS ANTHONY—May it please your honor, I am not arguing the question, but simply stating the reasons why sentence cannot, in justice, be pronounced against me. Your denial of my citizen's right to vote, is the denial of my right of consent as one of the governed, the denial of my right of representation as one of the taxed, the denial of my right to a trial by a jury of my peers, as an offender against law, therefore, the denial of my sacred rights to life, liberty, property and—

JUDGE HUNT—The Court cannot allow the prisoner to go on.

MISS ANTHONY—But your honor will not deny me this one and only poor privilege of protest against this high-handed outrage upon my citizen's rights. May it please the Court to remember that since the day of my arrest last November, this is the first time that either myself or any person of my disfranchised class has been allowed a word of defense before judge or jury—

JUDDE HUNT—The prisoner must sit down—the Court cannot allow it.

Miss Anthony—All of my prosecutors, from the 8th ward corner grocery politician, who entered the complaint, to the United States Marshal, Commissioner, District Attorney, District Judge, your honor on the bench, not one is my peer, but each and all are my political sovereigns; and had your honor submitted my case to the jury, as was clearly your duty, even then I should have had just cause of protest, for not one of those men was my peer; but, native or foreign born, white or black, rich or poor, educated or ignorant, awake or asleep, sober or drunk, each and every man of them was my political superior; hence, in no sense, my peer. Even, under such circumstances, a commoner of England, tried before a jury of Lords, would have far less cause to complain than should I, a woman, tried before a jury of men. Even my counsel, the Hon. Henry R. Selden, who has argued my cause so ably, so earnestly, so unanswerably before your honor, is my political sovereign. Precisely as no disfranchised person is entitled to sit upon a jury, and no woman is entitled to the franchise, so, none but a regularly admitted lawyer is allowed to practice in the courts, and no woman can gain admission to the bar—hence, jury, judge, counsel, must all be of the superior class.

Judge Hunt—The Court must insist—the prisoner has been tried according to the established forms of law.

Miss Anthony—Yes, your honor, but by forms of law all made by men, interpreted by men, administered by men, in favor of men, and against women; and hence, your honor's ordered verdict of guilty, against a United States citizen for the exercise of "*that citizen's right to vote,*" simply because that citizen was a woman and not a man. But, yesterday, the same man made forms of law, declared it a crime punishable with $1,000 fine and six months' imprisonment, for you, or me, or any of us, to give a cup of cold water, a crust of bread, or a night's shelter to a panting fugitive as he was tracking his way to Canada. And every man or woman in whose veins coursed a drop of human sympathy violated that wicked law, reckless of consequences, and was justified in so doing. As then, the slaves who got their freedom must take it over, or under, or through the unjust forms of law, precisely so, now, must women, to get their right to a voice in this government, take it; and I have taken mine, and mean to take it at every possible opportunity.

JUDGE HUNT—The Court orders the prisoner to sit down. It will not allow another word.

MISS ANTHONY—When I was brought before your honor for trial, I hoped for a broad and liberal interpretation of the Constitution and its recent amendments, that should declare all United States citizens under its protecting ægis—that should declare equality of rights the national guarantee to all persons born or naturalized in the United States. But failing to get this justice—failing, even, to get a trial by a jury *not* of my peers—I ask not leniency at your hands—but rather the full rigors of the law.

JUDGE HUNT—The Court must insist—

(Here the prisoner sat down.)

JUDGE HUNT—The prisoner will stand up.

(Here Miss Anthony arose again.)

The sentence of the Court is that you pay a fine of one hundred dollars and the costs of the prosecution.

MISS ANTHONY—May it please your honor, I shall never pay a dollar of your unjust penalty. All the stock in trade I possess is a $10,000 debt, incurred by publishing my paper—*The Revolution*—four years ago, the sole object of which was to educate all women to do precisely as I have done, rebel against your man-made, unjust, unconstitutional forms of law, that tax, fine, imprison and hang women, while they deny them the right of representation in the government; and I shall work on with might and main to pay every dollar of that honest debt, but not a penny shall go to this unjust claim. And I shall earnestly and persistently continue to urge all women to the practical recognition of the old revolutionary maxim, that "Resistance to tyranny is obedience to God."

JUDGE HUNT—Madam, the Court will not order you committed until the fine is paid.

INDICTMENT AGAINST BEVERLY W. JONES, EDWIN T. MARSH, AND WILLIAM B. HALL.

DISTRICT COURT OF THE UNITED STATES OF AMERICA, IN AND FOR THE NORTHERN DISTRICT OF NEW YORK.

At a stated Session of the District Court of the United States of America, held in and for the Northern District of New York, at the City Hall, in the city of Albany, in the said Northern District of New York, on the third Tuesday of January, in the year of our Lord one thousand eight hundred and seventy-three, before the Honorable Nathan H. Hall, Judge of the said Court, assigned to keep the peace of the said United States of America, in and for the said District, and also to hear and determine divers Felonies, Misdemeanors and other offences against the said United States of America, in the said District committed.

Brace Millerd,	Abram Kimmey,
James D. Wasson,	Derrick B. Van Schoonhoven,
Peter H. Bradt,	Wilhelmus Van Natten,
James McGinty,	James Kenney,
Henry A. Davis,	Adam Winne,
Loring W. Osborn,	James Goold,
Thomas Whitbeck,	Samuel S. Fowler,
John Mullen,	Peter D. R. Johnson,
Samuel C. Harris,	Patrick Carroll,
Ralph Davis,	
Matthew Fanning,	

good and lawful men of the said District, then and there sworn and charged to inquire for the said United States of America, and for the body of said District, do, upon their oaths, present, that at the City of Rochester, in the County of Monroe, in the Northern District of New York, on the 15th day of October, A. D. 1872, Beverly W. Jones, Edwin T. Marsh and William B. Hall were then and there Inspectors of Elections in and for the first election District of the eighth ward of said City of Rochester, duly elected, appointed, qualified and acting as such Inspectors.

And the Jurors aforesaid, upon their oaths aforesaid, do further present that on the day aforesaid, said Inspectors duly met at the place designated for holding a poll of an election to be had and held at and in said election District on the fifth day of November, A. D. 1872, for Representatives in the Congress of the United States, to-wit: a Representative in the Congress of the United States for the State of New York at large, and a Representative in the Congress of the United States for the Twenty-Ninth Congressional District of the State of New York, said first election District of said eighth ward then and there being a part of said Twenty-Ninth Congressional District of the State of

New York, and for other officers, and at said place on said day did then and there duly organize themselves as a board for the purpose of Registering the names of the legal voters of such District, and did then and there proceed to make a list of all persons entitled to vote at said election in said District, said list to constitute and to be known as the Registry of electors of said District.

And said Board of Inspectors again duly met on the Friday of the week preceding the day of said election, to-wit, on the first day of November, A. D. 1872, at the place designated for holding the poll of said election in and for said first election District, for the purpose of receiving and correcting said list, and for that purpose duly met at eight o'clock in the morning of the day aforesaid, at the place aforesaid, and remained in session until nine o'clock in the evening of that day; and for the purpose aforesaid, said Board of Inspectors again duly met at the place aforesaid, at eight o'clock in the morning of the day following, to-wit, the second day of November, A. D. 1872, and remained in session until nine o'clock in the evening of that day.

And the Jurors aforesaid, upon their oaths aforesaid, do further present that on the said second day of November, A. D. 1872, at the City of Rochester, in the County of Monroe, in the Northern District of New York, and within the jurisdiction of this Court, to-wit, at the place designated for holding the poll of said election for said Representatives in the Congress of the United States, and other officers in and for said first election District of said eighth ward as aforesaid, and between the hours of eight o'clock in the morning, and nine o'clock in the evening of said second day of November, A. D. 1872, Beverly W. Jones, Edwin T. Marsh and William B. Hall, being then and there Inspectors of Elections in and for said first election District of said eighth ward of said City of Rochester, duly elected, appointed, qualified and acting as such, and having then and there duly met for the purpose of revising and correcting said list of all persons entitled to vote at said election as aforesaid, known as the registry of electors for said election district, they, said Beverly W. Jones, Edwin T. Marsh and William B. Hall, *did then and there knowingly and wilfully register as a voter of said District, one Susan B. Anthony, she, said Susan B. Anthony then and there not being entitled to be registered as a voter of said District in that she, said Susan B. Anthony was then and there a person of the female sex, contrary to the form of the statute of the United States of America in such case made and provided, and against the peace of the United States of America and their dignity.*

Second Count: And the Jurors aforesaid, upon their oaths aforesaid, do further present that at the City of Rochester, in the County of Monroe, in the Northern District of New York, on the fifteenth day of October, A. D. 1872, Beverly W. Jones, Edwin T. Marsh and William B. Hall, were then and there Inspectors of Elections in and for the first election District of the eight ward of said City of Rochester, duly elected, appointed, qualified and acting as such.

And the Jurors aforesaid, upon their oaths aforesaid, do further present that on the day aforesaid, said Inspectors duly met at the place designated for the holding of the poll of an election to be had and held at and in said election District on the fifth day of November, A. D. 1872, for Representatives in the Congress of the United States, to-wit: a Representative in the Congress of the United States for the State of New York at large, and a Representative in the Congress of the United States for the Twenty-Ninth Congressional District of the State of New York, said first election district of said eighth ward then and there being a part of said Twenty-Ninth Congressional District of the State of New York, and for other officers, and at said place on said day, did then and there duly organize themselves as a Board for the purpose of

Registering the names of the legal voters of said District, and did then and there proceed to make a list of all persons entitled to vote at said election in said District, said list to constitute and to be known as the registry of electors of said District.

And said Board of Inspectors again duly met on the Friday of the week preceding the day of said election, to-wit, on the first day of November, A. D. 1872, at the place designated for holding the poll of said election in and for said first Election District, for the purpose of revising and correcting said list, and for that purpose duly met at eight o'clock in the morning of the day aforesaid, at the place aforesaid, and remained in session until nine o'clock in the evening of that day; and for the purpose aforesaid, said Board of Inspectors again duly met at the place aforesaid, at eight o'clock in the morning of the day following, to-wit, the second day of November, A. D. 1872, and remained in session until nine o'clock in the evening of that day.

And the Jurors aforesaid, upon their oaths aforesaid, do further present, that on the said first day of November, A. D. 1872, at the City of Rochester, in the County of Monroe, in the Northern District of New York, and within the jurisdiction of this Court, to-wit, at the place designated for holding the poll of said election for said Representatives in the Congress of the United States, and other officers in and for said first election District of said eighth ward of said City of Rochester, and between the hours of eight o'clock in the morning, and nine o'clock in the evening of said first day of November, A. D. 1872, Beverly W. Jones, Edwin T. Marsh and William B. Hall being then and there Inspectors of Elections in and for said first election District of said eighth ward of said City of Rochester, duly elected, appointed, qualified and acting as such as aforesaid, and having then and there duly met for the purpose of revising and correcting said list of all persons entitled to vote at said election as aforesaid, known as the Registry of electors for said election District, they, said Beverly W. Jones, Edwin T. Marsh and William B. Hall, *did then and there knowingly and wilfully register as voters of said District, certain persons, to-wit:* Susan B. Anthony, Sarah Truesdale, Mary Pulver, Mary Anthony, Ellen S. Baker, Margaret Leyden, Anna L. Moshier, Nancy M. Chapman, Lottie B. Anthony, Susan M. Hough, Hannah Chatfield, Mary S. Hibbard, Rhoda De Garmo, and Jane Cogswell, said persons then and there not being entitled to be Registered as voters of said District, in that each of said persons was then and there a person of the female sex, contrary to the form of the statute of the United States of America in such case made and provided, and against the peace of the United States of America and their dignity.

Third Count: And the Jurors aforesaid, upon their oaths aforesaid, do further present that Beverly W. Jones, Edwin T. Marsh and William D. Hall, of the City of Rochester, in the County of Monroe, with force and arms, &c., to-wit, at and in the first election District of the eighth ward of said City of Rochester, in the County of Monroe, in the Northern District of New York, and within the jurisdiction of this Court, heretofore, to-wit, on the fifth day of November, A. D. 1872, at an election duly held at and in the said first election District of the said eighth ward of said City of Rochester, in said County, and in said Northern District of New York, which said election was for Representatives in the Congress of the United States, to-wit, a Representative in the Congress of the United States for the State of New York at large, and a Representative in the Congress of the United States for the Twenty-Ninth Congressional District of the State of New York, said first election District of said eighth ward of said City of Rochester being then and there a part of said Twenty-Ninth Congressional District of State of New York, and said Beverly W. Jones,

Edwin T. Marsh, and William B. Hall, being then and there Inspectors of Elections in and for said first election District of said eighth ward of said City of Rochester, in said County of Monroe, duly elected, appointed, and qualified and acting as such, they, said Beverly W. Jones, Edwin T. Marsh, and William B. Hall, as such Inspectors of Elections, did then and there, to-wit, on the fifth day of November, A. D. 1872, at the first election District of the eighth ward of the City of Rochester, in the County of Monroe, in the Northern District of New York, and within the jurisdiction of this Court, knowingly and wilfully receive the votes of certain persons, and not then and there entitled to vote, to-wit: Susan B. Anthony, Sarah Truesdale, Mary Pulver, Mary Anthony, Ellen S. Baker, Margaret Leyden, Hannah L. Mosher, Nancy M. Chapman, Susan M. Hough, Guelma S. McLean, Hannah Chatfield, Mary S. Hibbard, Rhoda DeGarmo, and Jane Cogswell, each of said persons then and there being a person of the female sex, and then and there not entitled to vote, as they, said Beverly W. Jones, Edwin T. Marsh and William B. Hall then and there well knew, contrary to the form of the statute of the United States of America in such case made and provided, and against the peace of the United States of America and their dignity.

Fourth Count: And the Jurors aforesaid, upon their oaths aforesaid, do further present, that Beverly W. Jones, Edwin T. Marsh and William B. Hall, now, or late of Rochester, in the County of Monroe, with force and arms, &c., to-wit, at and in the first election District of the eighth ward of the City of Rochester, in the County of Monroe, in said Northern District of New York, and within the jurisdiction of this Court heretofore, to wit, on the fifth day of November, A. D. 1872, at an election duly held at and in the said first election District of said eighth ward of said City of Rochester, in said County of Monroe, in said Northern District of New York, which said election was for Representatives in the Congress of the United States, to-wit: a Representative in the Congress of the United States for the State of New York at large, and a Representative in the Congress of the United States for the Twenty-Ninth Congressional District of the State of New York, said first election District of said eighth ward being then and there a part of said Twenty-Ninth Congressional District, and they, said Beverly W. Jones, Edwin T. Marsh, and William B. Hall, being then and there Inspectors of Elections in and for said first election District of said eighth ward of said City of Rochester, in said County of Monroe, duly appointed, elected, qualified and acting as such, they said Beverly W. Jones, Edwin T. Marsh, and William B. Hall, did then and there, to-wit, at said first election District of said eighth ward of said City of Rochester, in said County of Monroe, in said Northern District of New York, on said fifth day of November, A. D. 1872, knowingly and wilfully receive the votes of certain persons for candidate for Representative in the Congress of the United States for the State of New York at large, and candidate for Representative in the Congress of the United States for the Twenty-Ninth Congressional District of the State of New York, said persons then and there not being entitled to vote for said Representatives in the Congress of the United States, viz.: Susan B. Anthony, Sarah Truesdale, Mary Pulver, Mary Anthony, Ellen S. Baker, Margaret Leyden, Hannah L. Mosher, Nancy M. Chapman, Lottie B. Anthony, Susan M. Hough, Guelma L. McLean, Hannah Chatfield, Mary S. Hibbard, Rhoda De Garmo and Jane Cogswell, each of said persons then and there being a person of the female sex, and then and there not entitled to vote for said Representatives in Congress, as they, said Beverly W. Jones, Edwin T. Marsh and William B. Hall, then and there well knew, contrary to the form of the statute of the United States of America in such case made and provided, against the peace of the United States of America and their dignity.

RICHARD CROWLEY,
Attorney of the United States, in and for the Northern District of New York.

(Endorsed.) January 22, 1873.

Jones and Marsh plead not guilty.

RICHARD CROWLEY,
U. S. Attorney.

Hall did not plead at all.

UNITED STATES CIRCUIT COURT.

NORTHERN DISTRICT OF NEW YORK.

THE UNITED STATES OF AMERICA

vs.

BEVERLY W. JONES, EDWIN T. MARSH, AND WILLIAM B. HALL.

HON. WARD HUNT, Presiding.

APPEARANCES.

For the United States:

HON. RICHARD CROWLEY,
U. S. District Attorney.

For the Defendants:

JOHN VAN VOORHIS, ESQ.

Tried at Canandaigua, Wednesday, June 18th, 1873, before Hon. Ward Hunt and a Jury.

Case opened in behalf of the U. S. by Mr. Crowley.

MR. VAN VOORHIS: I wish to raise some questions upon the indictment in this case. This indictment, I claim, is bad for two reasons, and should be quashed.

First—The Act of Congress under which it is framed, is invalid so far as it relates to this offence, because not authorized by the Constitution of the United States.

Second—There is no sufficient statement of any offence in the indictment.

First.

Congress has no power to pass laws for the punishment of Inspectors of Elections, elected or appointed under the laws of the State of New York, for receiving illegal votes, or registering as voters, persons who have no right to be registered.

No law of Congress defines the qualifications of voters in the several States. These are found only in the State Constitutions and Statutes. The offenses charged in the indictment are, that the defendants, being State officers, have violated the laws of the State. If it be so, they may be tried and punished in accordance with the State laws. No proposition can be clearer. If the United States can also punish them for the same offense, it follows that they may be twice indicted, tried, convicted and punished for one offense. A plea in a State Court, of a conviction and sentence, in a United States Court would constitute no bar or defense. (*12 Metcalf, 387, Commonwealth v. Peters,*) and the defendants might be punished twice for the same offense. This cannot be, and if the act in question be valid, the State of New York is ousted of jurisdiction. And where does Congress derive the power to pass laws to punish offenders against the laws of a

State? This case must be tried under the laws of the United States. Against those laws, no offense is charged to have been committed. Such power, if it exist, must be somewhere expressly granted, or it must be necessary in order to execute some power that is expressly granted.

The Act of Congress in question, became a law on May 31st, 1870. It is entitled—

"AN ACT TO ENFORCE THE RIGHT OF CITIZENS OF THE UNITED STATES TO VOTE IN THE SEVERAL STATES, AND FOR OTHER PURPOSES."

The indictment is found under the 19th section of the Act as it passed originally, and the 20th section as amended by the Act of February 28th, 1871.

The 19th Section, so far as it is necessary to quote it here, is as follows:

"*That if at any election for representatives or del-*
"*egates in the Congress of the United States any per-*
"*son shall knowingly* personate and vote, or attempt
"to vote, in the name of any other person, whether
"living or dead, or fictitious; or vote more than once
"at the same election for any candidate for the same
"office; or vote at a place where he may not be enti-
"titled to vote; *or vote without having a lawful right*
"*to vote,* * * * * *or knowingly and wilfully re-*
"*ceives the vote of any person not entitled to vote,* or
"refuses to receive the vote of any person entitled to
"vote; * * * * every such person shall be
"deemed guilty of a crime, and shall for such crime
"be liable to prosecution in any Court of the United
"States of competent jurisdiction, and on conviction
"thereof, shall be punished by a fine not exceeding
"five hundred dollars, or by imprisonment for a term
"not exceeding three years, or both, in the discretion
"of the Court, and shall pay the costs of prosecution."

Section 20, as amended, so far as pertinent, reads as follows:

"That if at any registration of voters for an election "for representatives or delegates in the Congress of "the United States, any person shall *knowingly* * * " * * hinder any person having a lawful right to "register, from duly exercising that right; or compel "or induce by any of such means, or other unlawful "means, ANY OFFICER OF REGISTRATION to admit to "registration any person not legally entitled thereto; " * * * *or if any such officer shall knowingly* "*and wilfully register as a voter any person not en-* "*titled to be registered*, or refuse so to register any "person entitled to be registered, * * * *every such* "*person shall be deemed guilty of a crime, and shall* "*be liable to prosecution and punishment therefor,* "*as provided in section 19 of said Act of May 31,* "*1870, for persons guilty of the crimes therein* "*specified.*"

No law of Congress describes the qualifications of voters in this State, or in any State.

Congress has provided no registry law. Therefore, what constitutes the offenses charged in this indictment, must be looked for in the laws of the State. By no Act of Congress can it be determined in what case a person votes, "*without having a right to vote.*" By no Act of Congress can it be determined when an Inspector of Election has received the vote of "*any person not entitled to vote,*" or has registered "*as a voter, any person not entitled to be registered.*" These are the offenses alleged in this indictment. They are penal offenses by the Statutes of New York. The jurisdiction of the State Courts over them is complete, and cannot be questioned.

By the Act of May 31, 1870, above cited, Congress has ordained, in legal effect, that if any person violates the penal Code of the State of New York, or any State, in respect of voting, he may be punished by the United States. And the offense is a variable quantity; what is a crime in one State under this Act, is a legal right and duty in another. A citizen of Rhode Island, for instance, who votes when not possessed in his own right, of an estate in fee simple—in fee tail, for life, or in reversion or remainder, of the value of $134 or upwards, may be convicted of a crime under this Act, and imprisoned in a State Prison. He voted in violation of the laws of his State. A citizen of New York votes under precisely similar circumstances, and with the same qualifications, and his act is a legal one, and he performs a simple duty. Any State may, by its Constitution and laws, permit women to vote. Had these defendants been acting as Inspectors of Elections in such State, their act would be no crime, and this indictment could not be sustained, for the only illegality alleged is, that the citizens whose votes were received were women, and therefore not entitled to vote.

The Act of Congress thus, is simply an Act to enforce the diverse penal statutes of the various States in relation to voting. In order to make a case, the United States must combine the federal law with the statutes of the State where the *venue* of the prosecution is laid.

Before the enactment of the 13th, 14th and 15th Amendments, it is not, and never was pretended, that Congress possessed any such power. Subdivision 1 of Section 2, of Article one of the Constitution, provides as follows:

"The House of Representatives shall be composed "of members chosen every second year by the people "of the several States; and the electors in each State "shall have the qualifications requisite for electors of "the most numerous branch of the State Legislature."

By this provision, what shall qualify a person to be an elector, is left entirely to the States. Whoever, in any State, is permitted to vote for members of the most numerous branch of its legislature, is also competent to vote for Representatives in Congress. The State might require a property qualification, or it might dispense with it. It might permit negroes to vote, or it might exclude them. It might permit women to vote, or even foreigners, and the federal constitution would not be infringed. If a State had provided a different qualification for an elector of Representatives in Congress, from that required of an elector of the most numerous branch of its Legislature, the power of the federal constitution might be invoked, and the law annuled. But never was the idea entertained, that this provision of the Constitution authorizes Congress to pass laws for the punishment of individuals in the States for illegal voting, or State returning officers for receiving illegal votes.

This power, if it exist, must be found in the recent Amendments to the U. S. Constitution.

I assume that your Honor will hold, as you did yesterday in Miss Anthony's case, that these amendments do not confer the right to vote upon citizens of the United States, and therefore not upon women. That decision is the law of this case. It follows necessarily from that decision, that these amendments have nothing to do with the right of voting, except so far as that right "*is denied or abridged by the United States, or by any State, on account of race, color, or previous condition of servitude.*"

The thirteenth article of the Amendments to the Constitution of the United States, in Section 1, ordains that "*neither slavery nor involuntary servitude, except as a punishment for crime, whereof the party shall have been duly convicted, shall exist within the United States, or any place subject to their jurisdiction.*"

Section 2, ordains that "*Congress shall have power to enforce this Article by appropriate legislation.*"

The fourteenth article of the Amendments to the Constitution of the United States, ordains in Section 1. "*All persons born or naturalized in the United States, and subject to the jurisdiction thereof, are citizens of the United States, and of the State where they reside. No State shall make or enforce any law, which shall abridge the privileges or immunities of citizens of the United States. Nor shall any State deprive any person of life, liberty or property, without due process of law, nor deny to any person within its jurisdiction, the equal protection of the laws.*"

Section five enacts, "*The Congress shall have power to enforce by appropriate legislation, the provisions of this Article.*"

The fifteenth article of Amendment to the Constitution ordains in its first section, that "That the right "of citizens of the United States to vote, shall not be "denied or abridged by the United States or by any "State, on account of race, color or previous condi- "tion of servitude."

Section two enacts, that "*The Congress shall have "power to enforce this Article by appropriate leg- "islation.*"

These are the provisions of the Constitution relied on to support the legislation of Congress now before this Court. Some features of that legislation may be constitutional and valid. Whether this be so or not, it is not necessary now to determine. The question here is, has Congress, by either of these amendments, been clothed with the power, to pass laws to punish inspectors of elections in this State for receiving the votes of women?

The thirteenth amendment simply abolishes slavery, and authorizes such legislation as shall be necessary to make that enactment effectual.

The power in question is not found there.

The fourteenth amendment defines who are citizens of the United States, and prohibits the States from making or enforcing "*any law which shall abridge the privileges or immunities*" of such citizens.

Either the right to votes is one of the "*privileges or immunities*" of the United States citizen, which the states are forbidden to abridge, or it is not. If it is, then the women whose votes these defendants received, being citizens of the United States, and in every other way qualified to vote, possessed the right to vote, and their votes were rightfully received. If it is not, the the fourteenth amendment confers no power upon Congress, to legislate on the subject of voting in the States. There is no other clause or provision of that amendment which can by any possibility confer such power—a power which cannot be implied, but which, if it exist, must be expressly given in some part of the Constitution, or clearly needed to carry into effect some power that is expressly given.

No such power is conferred by the fifteenth amendment. That amendment operates upon the States and upon the United States, and not upon the citizen. "The right of citizens of the United States to vote, shall not be denied or abridged by "'THE UNITED STATES OR BY ANY STATE."' The terms "*United States*" and "State," as here used, mean the government of the United States and of the States. They do not apply to individuals or to offenses committed by individuals, but only to acts done by the State or the United States.

But at any rate, the operation of this amendment, and the power given to Congress to enforce it, is limited to offenses committed in respect of depriving persons of the right to vote because of their "*race, color, or previous condition of servitude.*"

This is not such a case. There is no ground for saying that these defendants have committed any offense against the spirit or the letter of the fifteenth amendment, or any legitimate legislation for its enforcement.

Congress cannot make laws to regulate the duties of Inspectors, and it cannot inflict a penalty.

Second.

No offense is stated in the indictment.

The first count in the indictment is for knowingly and wilfully registering as a voter, Susan B. Anthony. This count is under Section 26 of the Act of May 31, 1870, as amended by the Act of February 28, 1871.

The indictment contains no averment that the defendants were "*officers of registration*," and charged with the duty of making a correct registry of voters. It simply alleges that they were *Inspectors of Elections*. What that means, the indictment does not inform us. It is not an office defined by the Acts of Congress upon which this indictment was found, nor has the Court any information of which it can take notice as to what are the duties of such officers. In the absence of any claim in the indictment to that effect, the Court will not presume the existence of so important a circumstance against the defendants, and therefore this count of the indictment must fail.

2. The second count is for the same offense, and obnoxious to the same objection. The only variation being that the first count charges the illegal registry of one woman, and the second, fourteen.

3. The third count charges that the defendants, being inspectors of elections, received the votes of fourteen women who had no right to vote, wrongfully.

This count does not allege that it was the duty of the defendants to receive or count the votes. It simply alleges that they were Inspectors of Election. Their duties as such are not stated. It is not alleged that as such inspectors they were charged with the duty of receiving and counting votes. It is not claimed by the indictment that these votes were counted or put into the ballot box—or affected the result. The defendants simply received the votes. What they did with them, does not appear. Any bystander, who had received these votes, could be convicted under this indictment as well as they.

WILLIAM F. MORRISON, a witness called in behalf of the United States, testified as follows:

Examined by Mr. Crowley:

Q. Where did you live, in November, 1872?
A. City of Rochester.
Q. Where do you live now?
A. Same place.
Q. Did you occupy any official position in the month of November, 1872?
A. I did.
Q. And do you now?
A. Yes, sir.
Q. What is it?
A. City Clerk.
Q. Have you any registration lists and poll lists of the 1st Election District, 8th Ward, City of Rochester, in your possession?
A. I have.
Q. Will you produce them?

[Witness produces two books.]

Q. Do you know the defendants, Beverly W. Jones, Edwin T. Marsh, and Wm. B. Hall, or any them?
A. I know them all.
Q. Do you know their hand-writing?
A. I cannot say that I do.
Q. What are those books you hold in your hand?

A. The register of the Board of Registry, and the poll list kept on election day.

Q. In what district?

A. 1st election district of the 8th Ward.

Q. By whom were those books left in your office, if by any one?

A. To the best of my knowledge, they were left by Beverly W. Jones, Chairman of the Board of Inspectors.

Q. By whom do they purport to be signed?

A. Beverly W. Jones, Wm. B. Hall, and Edwin T. Marsh.

Q. Is there a certificate attached to them, purporting to show what they are?

Q. There is a certificate attached to the register, but not to the poll list.

Q. Please read the certificate attached to the registration list.

A. "We, the undersigned, composing the Board of Registry for the first district, 8th Ward, City of Rochester, do certify that the foregoing is a correct list of the voters in said district, so far as the same is known to us. Dated Nov. 2d, 1872."

Q. In what Congressional District was the first election district of the 8th Ward, in November, 1872?

A. 29th.

Q. Was there an election for Members of Congress for that district, and for Members of Congress at Large for the State, held in that ward and election district, last November?

A. Yes, sir.

Q. And candidates voted for for both of those officers by those who saw fit to vote for them?

A. Yes, sir.

Q. What day was the election?

A. 5th day of November.

MR. CROWLEY: We offer the poll list and the registration of voters in evidence.

[Poll list marked Ex. "A." Registration list, marked Ex. "B."]

[This witness was not cross-examined.]

SYLVESTER LEWIS, a witness sworn in behalf of the United States, testified as follows:

Examined by MR. CROWLEY:

Q. Where did you live in November, 1872?
A. In the city of Rochester.
Q. Do you know the defendants, Jones, Marsh and Hall?
A. I do.
Q. Do you know whether or not they acted as a Board of Registry for the registration of voters in the first election district, 8th ward, City of Rochester, preceding the last general election?
A. I know they acted at the November election.
Q. Did they act as a Board of Registry preceding the election?
A. Yes, sir.
Q. Was you present on any day when they were registering voters?
A. I was present on Friday mostly, and on Saturday.
Q. Were all three of these defendants there?
A. They were the most of the time.
Q. Receiving the names of persons who claimed to be entitled to vote?
A. Yes, sir.
Q. And taking a registration list?
A. Yes, sir.
Q. Did you see Miss Anthony and other ladies there upon that day?
A. I saw Miss Anthony there on the first day, and other ladies.
Q. Did you see there, upon that day, the following named persons: Susan B. Anthony, Sarah Truesdell, Mary Pulver, Mary Anthony, Ellen S. Baker, Margaret Leyden, Ann S. Mosher, Nancy M. Chapman,

Lottie B. Anthony, Susan M. Hough, Hannah Chatfield, Mary S. Hibbard, Rhoda DeGarmo, Jane Cogswell.

A. I saw a number of them; I didn't see the whole of them.

Q. Do you know by sight, any of those persons whose names I have read?

A. I know a number of them.

Q. Did you see a number of them there?

A. I did.

Q. Did you see any of them register on that day?

A. I did.

Q. Have you a list of those that you saw register?

A. I have, (producing a paper.)

Q. Please state to the Jury, those that you saw register on that day.

A. I can hardly recollect which day they registered.

Q. Either of the days preceding the election, when this Board was in session.

A. Rhoda DeGarmo, Mary Anthony, Sarah C. Truesdell, Susan M. Hough, Mrs. M. E. Pulver.

By Mr. Van Voorhis:

Q. What paper are you reading from?

A. From a memorandum I made at the time—No, it is a paper that was given on the last day of registry.

Q. A paper that you made yourself?

A. The names that I took.

Q. On the last day of registry?

A. Yes, sir.

By Mr. Crowley:

Q. State them.

A. The names of the parties that I found on the poll list as having registered; I didn't see them all register myself, but I did a good portion of them.

Q. I am asking you to state who you saw register, I don't ask you who were registered before your attention was called to the list.

A. Well, I saw Rhoda DeGarmo register; Miss Mary Anthony, Sarah C. Truesdell, Susan M. Hough; I think I saw Nancy M. Chatfield register; Mrs. Margaret Leyden, Mrs. M. E. Pulver; those I recollect; I was better acquainted with those than with the others.

Q. At the time you saw these ladies register, were the three inspectors, Hall, Jones, and Marsh present?

A. Some of the time I saw all three, I think, there; at other times I saw but two of them; sometimes Hall and Jones, sometimes Marsh and Jones, sometimes Hall and Marsh; I think they took turns when they went to dinner.

Q. On the day of election were you at the polls?

A. I was.

Q. Did you see any of these women vote on the day of election?

A. I did.

Q. Were these defendants present when their votes were received?

A. They were.

Q. And did they receive their votes?

A. They did.

Q. Who did you see vote, or offer their votes upon the day of election?

A. Susan B. Anthony, Mrs. McLean, Rhoda De Garmo, Mary Anthony, Ellen S. Baker, Sarah C. Truesdell, Mrs. Hough, Mrs. Mosher, Mrs. Leyden, Mrs. Pulver. I recollect seeing those ladies; in fact, I think I saw the whole of them vote with the exception of two, but I will not be positive on that point.

Q. But you saw those whose names you have given?

A. Yes, sir.

Q. Do you know how many tickets they voted, or offered to the inspectors?

A. I think they voted four tickets.

Q. Do you know how these tickets were endorsed, or what they were called?

A. I was not near enough to see the endorsement; I noticed which boxes they went into.

Q. Upon the day of election were the defendants Jones, Marsh, and Hall, acting as inspectors of election?

A. Yes, sir.

Q. Receiving votes?

A. Yes, sir.

Q. And were acting as inspectors of election when these ladies voted?

A. Yes, sir.

Q. About what time in the day, or what time in the morning was it that these ladies voted?

A. I think there had been but a very few votes received in the morning when a number of them voted.

Q. Well, was it about 5 o'clock in the morning—very early?

A. No, sir; not so early as that; the probability is that there was not over 20 or 25 votes received before they presented theirs.

Conceded: That the women named in the indictment were women on the 5th day of November, 1872.

Cross-Examination by Mr. Van Voorhis:

Q. Which of those persons did you see register?

A. Mrs. Hough, Mrs. Pulver, Mrs. Truesdell, Mrs. Leyden.

Q. Do you swear you saw Mrs. Leyden register?

A. I think I did.

Q. Take a second thought and see if you are willing to say you saw her register—please look off that paper. Do you recollect seeing those persons register, or do you suppose they did, because you find it on a paper there?

A. No, sir; I recollect seeing pretty much all of them on my list with the exception of one or two; I won't be fully positive I saw Mrs. Leyden register; I saw her vote.

Q. Did you go to Mrs. Leyden's house and advise her to go and register?

A. I don't think I did.

The Court: That is not important.

Q. Do you recollect seeing any others register except those you have now mentioned?

A. I think I saw Mary Anthony.

Q. Any other?

A. Mrs. Chapman.

Q. Can you recollect this without looking at that paper?

A. Well, the object in looking at that paper is to try to refresh my memory on which day they registered.

Q. Does that paper contain dates?

A. No, sir; it contains the names of all those who registered.

Q. You copied that paper from the registry, didn't you?

A. They were copied by Hall at the time of the election, and handed to me.

Q. What was your business at the registry at that time?

A. I had a poll list; I was checking parties that I supposed had a legal right to vote.

Q. What sort of a poll list?

Objected to as immaterial.

THE COURT: It is only competent as a test of his knowledge.

A. I had canvassed the ward and taken a list of all the voters in the first district; all those that I supposed would be entitled to vote.

Q. You had canvassed the ward in the employment of somebody?

Objected to as immaterial.

Q. How many of these people did you see vote?

A. I think I saw the whole of them vote, with the exception of Mrs. Hough and Mrs. Cogswell.

Q. Who took Miss Anthony's vote?

A. Mr. Jones.

Q. Were both the other inspectors present when he took it?

A. I believe they were.

Q. Did Jones take all of the votes of those persons whose names you have on your list?

A. I don't think he did.

Q. Who took any others that you saw?

A. I saw Mr. Hall take some of the ballots.

Q. How many?

A. I could n't tell how many.

Q. Did you see him take more than one?

A. I don't know as I did.

Q. Do you know whose it was?

A. If I recollect right, it was Mrs. DeGarmo's.

Q. At that time was Jones there?

A. No, I believe Jones had stepped out.

Q. Hall received the vote on account of Jones being absent?

A. I believe so.

Q. Jones' position was at the window receiving votes?

A. Yes, sir.

Q. Who put them in the boxes?

A. Jones and Hall.

Q. You were not near enough to see what these ballots were?

A. No, sir.

Q. How many ballot boxes were there?

A. Six, if I recollect right.

Q. And six tickets voted at that poll?

A. Six tickets altogether; there was the Constitutional Amendment voted at that election.

Q. Did you observe which boxes the tickets of these persons were put into?

A. I did.

Q. Which were they?

A. I think that the ballots that these ladies voted.

Q. I don't want what you think; I want what you know.

A. Well, they went into those boxes; Member of Congress, Member at Large.

Q. Were there two boxes for Congressmen?

A. I think there was; I am not quite positive; I rather think I am mistaken about that.

Q. Well, give us what you know about the boxes?

A. The most that I know about is, that the remark was made by the inspector that they voted the four tickets.

Q. You heard the remark made that they voted four tickets; who made that remark?

A. Mr. Jones or Mr. Hall; when they passed their ballots they would say, "They vote all four tickets; no Constitutional Amendment voted."

Q. That was the practice of the inspector, no matter who voted?

A. Yes, sir.

Q. Then you didn't see the tickets as they went into the boxes?

A. No, sir.

Q. You can't swear which boxes they went into?

A. I understood from the inspectors that they voted all the tickets with the exception of the Constitutional Amendment.

Q. I don't ask for any conversation; I ask for what you know by what you saw.

A. Well, I was n't near enough to read the tickets.

Q. Did you hear either of the inspectors say anythiug about it?

A. I did.

Q. Which one?

A. I heard the inspector that would be at the window where the ballots would be received.

Q. Name him.

A. I heard Mr. Jones say that they voted the four tickets.

Q. Was that all he said?

A. Well, he would declare it in this way; sometimes he would say, "They vote all the tickets with the exception of the Amendment;" that is the way he generally declared it.

Q. I want to get at what he said when these votes were taken?

A. He didn't at all times declare the ticket voted.

Q. Are you willing to testify that you recollect distinctly, anything that was said by either of the inspectors when these ladies voted?

A, Most decidedly; I heard Jones say that they voted the Congressional ticket; I heard him say that they voted all the tickets.

Q. At the time they voted?

A. The question would be asked what tickets they voted, and he would say, "All the tickets with the exception of the Amendment."

Q. Did he mention the Congressional ticket?

A. I think he did.

Q. Do you recollect that he did?

A. My impression is that he said so; I can't say positively.

Q. Did you say anything there, about getting twenty women to vote?

Objected to as immaterial.

MR. VAN VOORHIS: I propose to show that this witness said to parties there that he would go and get twenty Irish women to vote, to offset these votes.

Objected to as immaterial.

Objection sustained.

WILLIAM F. MORRISON recalled.

Examined by MR. CROWLEY:

Q. Please point out the following names, if you find them in the registration list: Susan B. Anthony?

A. I find it.

Q. Sarah Truesdell?

A. Sarah C. Truesdell.
Q. Mary Pulver?
A. M. P. Pulver.
Q. Mary Anthony?
A. I find it.
Q. Ellen S. Baker?
A. Yes, sir; I have it.
Q. Margaret Leyden?
A. Margaret L. Leyden.
Q. Ann S. Mosher?
A. Hannah L. Mosher.
Q. Nancy M. Chapman?
A. Nancy M. Chapman.
Q. Lottie B. Anthony?
A. Lottie B. Anthony.
Q. Susan M. Hough?
A. Susan M. Hough.
Q. Hannah Chatfield?
A. Hannah Chatfield.
Q. Mary S. Hibbard?
A. Mary S. Hibbard.
Q. Rhoda De Garmo?
A. I don't find any such name; I find Robert De Garmo and Elias De Garmo.
Q. Jane Cogswell?
A. Jane Cogswell.
Q. Now turn to the names of voters contained in the list copied upon election day; do you find the name of Susan B. Anthony upon that list?
A. I do.
Q. Sarah Truesdell?
A. Yes, sir.
Q. Mary Pulver?
A. Yes, sir.
Q. Mary Anthony?
A. Yes, sir.
Q. Mary S. Baker?
A. Yes, sir.
Q. Margaret Leyden?
A. Yes, sir

Q. Ann S. Mosher?
A. Hannah L. Mosher.
Q. Nancy Chapman?
A. Yes, sir.
Q. Lottie B. Anthony?
A. Yes, sir.
Q. Susan M. Hough?
A. Yes, sir.
Q. Hannah Chatfield?
A. Yes, sir.
Q. Mary S. Hibbard?
A. Yes, sir.
Q. Rhoda De Garmo?
A. I find Mrs. Rosa De Garmo.
Q. Jane Cogswell?
A. Yes, sir.
Q. Upon the list copied by the inspectors upon the day of election, is there any heading purporting to show what tickets these people voted?
A. Yes, sir.
Q. Please state from the heading what tickets it purports to show they voted?
A. The first column is Electoral; the second, State; the third, Congress; the fourth, Assembly; the fifth, Constitutional Amendment.
Q. Please look and see which of those tickets the list purports to show that they voted?

MR. VAN VOORHIS: I object to any marks upon that book which the witness didn't make, as any evidence that these persons voted for members of Congress.

By THE COURT:

Q. What is the statement there?
A. After the name of Miss Susan B. Anthony in the column of electors there is a small, straight mark.

MR. VAN VOORHIS: I object to that, as not evidence of what these votes were.

THE COURT: I think it is competent.

By MR. CROWLEY:

Q. State, Mr. Morrison?

A. Opposite each of the names that I have read there are checks, showing that they voted Electoral, State, Congressional and Assembly tickets—four tickets.

Q. There are a large number of the inspectors' books of the last election filed with you as City Clerk, are there not?

A. Yes, sir.

Q. Do you know what the custom or habit is of copying these books when people vote?

Objected to.

Q. What custom the inspectors have of indicating what tickets a person votes when he offers his vote?

Objected to. Question withdrawn.

Cross-Examination by MR. VAN VOORHIS.

Q. All you know about these tickets or that book, is what appears on the face of it, is it not?

A. Yes, sir; that is all.

Q. You don't know who made those straight marks?

A. I don't.

Q. Or why they were made, so far as you have any knowledge?

A. No, sir.

Q. Do you know what those letters are? [Pointing on the book.]

A. Preliminary oath and general oath, I should say.

Q. You would say that to each of these persons the preliminary oath was administered, and also the general oath?

A. Yes, sir; it so shows here.

Mrs. Margaret Leyden, a witness called in behalf of the United States, having been duly affirmed, testified as follows:

Examined by Mr. Crowley:

Q. Did you reside in the City of Rochester in the month of November, 1872?
A. Yes, sir.
Q. Did you reside in the 8th ward?
A. I did.
Q. In the first election district of that ward?
A. I did.
Q. Was your name registered before the election which took place on the 5th of November, 1872?
A. It was.
Q. By whom?
A. I think Mr. Jones; in fact, all three of the inspectors were there.
Q. Did you, upon the 5th day of November, vote?
A. I did.
Q. Who received your vote?
A. Mr. Jones.
Q. Were the other inspectors there at the time?
A. Yes, sir.
Q. Did you vote for a candidate for Congress?
A. I did.

Cross-Examination by Mr. Van Voorhis:

Q. Was Mr. Lewis there when you registered?
A. Mr. Lewis was not there.
Q. Do you recollect who took your vote?
A. I think Mr. Jones took it; I know he did.
Q. Was your ballot folded up?
A. It was.
Q. Could any person read it, or see what you voted, or who you voted for?
A. No one but my husband.
Q. He saw it before you voted?
A. Yes, sir.

Q. Was your husband present when you voted?

Objected to as immaterial.

A. He was.
Q. No one had seen your ballot except your husband before you handed it in?
A. No, sir.
Q. And when you handed it in it was folded, so that no one could see it?
A. It was.

THE COURT: What is the object of this?

MR. VAN VOORHIS: The District Attorney inquired if she voted a certain ticket, and assumes to charge these inspectors with knowing what she voted. It is to show that the ticket being folded, the inspector could not see what was in it.

Q. In voting, did you believe that you had a right to vote, and vote in good faith?

Objected to as immaterial.

Objection sustained.

Re-Direct Examination by MR. CROWLEY:

Q. You have heard me name the different persons, have you not, when I asked Mr. Morrison questions?
A. Yes, sir.
Q. Were these people, or any of them, present, and were they registered at the same time you were?
A. Some of them were present.
Q. Who?
A. Mrs. Lottie B. Anthony; there was one lady that registered who didn't vote; I think Mrs. Anthony was the only lady that was present that voted; I can't recollect any more names.
Q. Who of these ladies were present when you voted and voted with you, if any?

A. Miss Susan B. Anthony, Mrs. Pulver, Mrs. Mosher, Mrs. Lottie B. Anthony, Miss Mary Anthony, Miss Baker, Mrs. Chapman.
Q. Did they all vote on that occasion?
A. They did.

Re-Cross Examination by MR. VAN VOORHIS.

Q. Mrs. Lottie B. Anthony is the wife of Alderman Anthony?
A. Yes, sir.

United States rests.

Case opened in behalf of the defendants by Mr. VAN VOORHIS.

BEVERLY W. JONES, one of the defendants, having been duly sworn as a witness in his own behalf, testified as follows:

Examined by MR. VAN VOORHIS.

Q. Mr. Jones, where do you reside?
A. Eighth ward, city of Rochester.
Q. What is your age?
A. Twenty-five last spring.
Q. Are you one of the defendants in this indictment?
A. Yes, sir.
Q. Were you inspector of election in the 8th ward?
A. Yes, sir.
Q. Which district?
A. First district.
Q. Were you elected or appointed?
A. Elected.
Q. By the people of the ward?
A. Yes, sir.
Q. Were you present at the Board of Registry when Miss Anthony and others appeared there and demanded to be registered?
A. I was.

Q. Won't you state what occurred there?

A. Miss Anthony and two other ladies came into the room; Miss Anthony asked if this was the place where they registered the names of voters; I told her it was; she said she would like to have her name registered; I told her I didn't think we could register her name; it was contrary to the Constitution of the State of New York; she said she didn't claim any rights under the Constitution of the State of New York; she claimed her rights under the Constitution of the United States; under an amendment to the Constitution; she asked me if I was conversant with the 14th amendment; I told her I had read it and heard of it several times.

Q. Before you go further, state who was present at that time?

A. William B. Hall and myself were the only inspectors; Mr. Marsh was not there; Daniel J. Warner, the United States Supervisor, Silas J. Wagner, another United States Supervisor, and a United States Marshal.

Q. State which one of these was Republican, and which one Democratic.

A. Silas J. Wagner, Republican; Daniel J. Warner, Democratic.

Q. Now go on.

A. She read the 14th amendment to the Constitution of the United States; while she was reading the amendment and discussing different points, Mr. Daniel J. Warner said—

Mr. Crowley: I submit to the Court that it is entirely immaterial what either Warner or Wagner said.

The Court: I don't see that that is competent in any view of the case.

Q. (By the Court). Was your objection to registering Miss Anthony on the ground that she was a woman?

A. I said it was contrary to the Constitution of the State of New York, and I didn't think that we could register her.

Q. (By the Court.) On what ground was that?
A. Well, on the ground that she was a woman.

By MR. VAN VOORHIS:

Q. You may proceed and state what occurred there?
A. Mr. Warner said—

Objected to.

THE COURT: I don't think that is competent, what Warner said:

MR. VAN VOORHIS: The district attorney has gone into what occurred at that time, and I ask to be permitted to show *all* that occurred at the time of the registry; this offense was committed there; it is a part of the *Res Gesta;* all that occurred at the moment Miss Anthony presented herself and had her name put upon the registry.

THE COURT: I don't think that is competent.

MR. VAN VOORHIS: I ask to show what occurred at the time of registry.

THE COURT: I don't think it is competent to stat what Warner or Wagner advised.

MR. VAN VOORHIS: So that the question may appear squarely in the case I offer to show what was said and done at the time Miss Anthony and the other ladies registered, by them, the inspectors, and the federal Supervisors, Warner and Wagner, in their presence, in regard to that subject.

THE COURT: I exclude it.

MR. VAN VOORHIS: Does that exclude all conversations that occurred there with any persons?

THE COURT: It excludes anything of that character

on the subject of advising them. Your case is just as good without it as with it.

Mr. Van Voorhis: I didn't offer it in view of the advice, but to show precisely what the operation of the minds of these inspectors was at that time, and what the facts are.

The Court: It is not competent.

By Mr. Van Voorhis:

Q. Were you present on the day of election?
A. Yes, sir.
Q. Did you receive the votes of these persons?
A. I did.
Q. How many ballot boxes were there there?
A. Six.
Q. What position did you occupy during the day?
A. Chairman of the Board.
Q. Did you stand at the window and receive the votes?
A. Most of the time I did.
Q. Were those ballots which you received from them folded?
A. They were.
Q. Did you or any of the inspectors see or know the contents of any of the ballots?

Mr. Crowley: If your Honor please, I submit it is entirely immaterial whether these inspectors saw the names upon the ballots.

The Court: I have excluded that already. It is not competent. It is proved that they put in votes, and it is proved by one of the ladies that she did vote for a candidate for Congress.

Mr. Van Voorhis: I propose to show by the witness that he didn't know the contents of any ballot, and didn't see it.

The Court: That will be assumed. He could not do it with any propriety.

By Mr. Van Voorhis:

Q. Did either one of the inspectors object to receiving the votes of the women at the polls?

A. Yes, sir.

Q. Which one?

A. William B. Hall.

Q. Did he take any part in receiving votes, and, if so, state what part?

A. I believe that he took the ballot of one lady, and placed it in the box. I stepped out, I believe, for a few moments.

Q. Did it to accommodate you while you stepped out?

A. Yes, sir.

Q. On the day of registry did the inspectors as a board decide unanimously to register these votes, all three of you consenting?

A. We did.

Q. When you came to receive the votes, Hall dissented?

A. He did, sir.

Q. But the other two were a majority, and he was overruled; was this the way it was, or wasn't there anything in form said about it?

A. He was overruled; I felt it my duty to take the ballots.

Q. In receiving those ballots did you act honestly in accordance with your sense of duty, and in accordance with your best judgment?

A. I did.

By Mr. Crowley:

Q. All three of the inspectors agreed in receiving these names for registration, did they not?

A. Yes, sir.

By Mr. Van Voorhis:

Q. I meant to have asked you in reference to the

challenges; state whether or not challenges were entered against these voters prior to the day of election?

A. There was.

Q. On their presenting their votes, what was done?

A. I told Miss Anthony, when she offered her vote, that she was challenged; she would have to swear her ballot in if she insisted upon voting; she said she insisted upon voting, and I presented her the Bible and administered to her the preliminary oath, which she took. I turned to the gentleman that challenged her, and asked him if he still insisted upon her taking the general oath.

Q. Were questions asked her?

A. There were, after taking the preliminary oath.

Q. In accordance with the instruction?

A. Yes, sir.

Q. Go on.

A. I turned to the gentleman that challenged her, and asked him if he still insisted on his challenge; he said he did; I told her she would have to take the general oath; I administered the general oath, and she took it.

Q. Was that done in each case of the women who voted?

A. It was.

By Mr. Crowley:

Q. As I understand you, all three of the inspectors agreed in permitting these people to be registered?

A. They didn't at first.

Q. Well, they did before they were registered, did they not?

A. They did before their names were put upon the book.

Q. And when they voted, yourself and Mr. Marsh were in favor ot receiving the votes, and Hall was opposed to receiving the votes?

A. Yes, sir.

By Mr. Van Voorhis:

Q. Did you suppose at that time that the law required you to take their votes?

Objected to. Sustained.

By Mr. Crowley:

Q. Did you have two meetings for the purpose of registration prior to election?
A. Yes, sir.
Q. Upon the days fixed by the laws of the State of New York?
A. Yes, sir.
Q. You made a list or registry, did you not, upon those days?
A. We did.
Q. Upon the day of election you had a list of voters?
A. Yes, sir.
Q. Those produced here to-day are the lists kept upon that occasion, are they not?
A. (After looking at Exhibits A. and B.) Those are the books.

By The Court:

Q. Did these ladies vote the Congressional ticket, all of them?
A. I couldn't swear to that.
Q. Look at the book as to that.
A. It does not tell for certain; the clerks may have made a mistake in making these marks; they do very often.
Q. Did you make any of the entries in that book?
A. No, sir; a clerk appointed by me did it.

By Mr. Crowley:

Q. When you counted up your votes at night, when the polls closed, did you compare your votes with the list?

A. Yes, sir.

Q. Did you find it correct?

A. We found it fell short of the poll list several ballots; I can't tell how many.

Q. Do you know whether it fell short on members of Congress?

A. Yes, sir, it did.

Q. Did you make a certificate and return of that fact?

A. Yes, sir; the certificate was filed in the Clerk's office.

EDWIN T. MARSH, one of the defendants, having been duly affirmed as a witness in his own behalf, testified as follows:

Examined by MR. VAN VOORHIS:

Q. Were you one of the inspectors of the 8th ward?

A. I was.

Q. How was you appointed?

A. I was appointed by the Common Council just before the first meeting of the board.

Q. What is your age?

A. I am 33.

Q. Did you hear the statement of Mr. Jones?

A. I did.

Q. To save time, I will ask you whether that was substantially correct as you understand it?

A. Yes, sir.

Q. Now, I will ask you the question if, in registering and receiving these votes, you believed that the law required you to do it, and yon acted conscientiously and honestly?

Objected to.

THE COURT: Put the question as you did to the other witness—whether in receiving these votes he acted honestly and according to the best of his judgment.

By MR. VAN VOORHIS:

Q. Answer that question, please?
A. I most assuredly did.

[This witness was not cross-examined.]

WILLIAM C. STORRS, a witness sworn in behalf of the defendants, testified as follows:

Examined by MR. VAN VOORHIS:

Q. Where do you reside?
A. City of Rochester.
Q. What office do you hold?
A. United States Commissioner.
Q. How long have you held that office?
A. Fifteen years.
Q. Do you know these defendants, Jones and Marsh?
A. I do, sir.
Q. Was any application made to you, by any person, at any time, for a warrant against them for this offence?

Objected to.

MR. VAN VOORHIS: If the counsel objects I will not insist upon the evidence.

[This witness was not cross-examined.]

SUSAN B. ANTHONY, called as a witness in behalf of the defendants.

MISS ANTHONY: I would like to know if the testimony of a person who has been convicted of a crime, can be taken?

THE COURT: They call you as a witness, madam.

The witness, having been duly affirmed, testified as follows:

Examined by Mr. Van Voorhis :

Q. Miss Anthony, I want you to state what occurred at the Board of Registry, when your name was registered ?

A. That would be very tedious, for it was full an hour.

Q. State generally what was done, or what occupied that hour's time ?

Objected to.

Q. Well, was the question of your right to be registered a subject of discussion there ?

A. It was.

Q. By and between whom ?

A. Between the supervisors, the inspectors, and myself.

Q. State, if you please, what occurred when you presented yourself at the polls on election day ?

A. Mr. Hall decidedly objected—

Mr. Crowley : I submit to the Court that unless the counsel expects to change the version given by the other witnesses, it is not necessary to take up time.

The Court : As a matter of discretion, I don't see how it will be of any benefit. It was fully related by the others, and doubtless correctly.

Mr. Crowley : It is not disputed.

The Witness : I would like to say, if I might be allowed by the Court, that the general impression that I swore I was a male citizen, is an erroneous one.

By Mr. Van Voorhis :

Q. You took the two oaths there, did you ?

A. Yes, sir.

By The Court:

Q. You presented yourself as a female, claiming that you had a right to vote?

A. I presented myself not as a female at all, sir; I presented myself as a citizen of the United States. I was called to the United States ballot box by the 14th amendment, not as a female, but as a citizen, and I went there.

Mr. Van Voorhis: We have a number of witnesses to prove what occurred at the time of registry, and what advice was given by these federal supervisors, but under your Honor's ruling it is not necessary for us to call them. Inasmuch as Mr. Hall is absent, I ask permission to put in his evidence as he gave it before the Commissioners.

Mr. Crowley: I have not read it, your Honor, but I am willing they should use so much of it as is competent under your Honor's ruling.

The Court: Will it change the case at all, Mr. Van Voorhis?

Mr. Van Voorhis: It only varies it a little as to Hall. He stated that he depended in consenting to the registry, upon the advice of Mr. Warner, who was his friend, and upon whom he looked as a political father.

The Court: I think you have all the question that any evidence could give you in the case. These men have sworn that they acted honestly, and in accordance with their best judgment. Now, if that is a defense, you have it, and it will not make it any stronger to multiply evidence.

Mr. Van Voorhis: I suppose it will be conceded that Hall stands in the same position as to his motives?

Mr. Crowley: Yes; we have no evidence to offer upon that question at all.

Evidence closed.

Mr. Van Voorhis addressed the Court at some length, as follows:

May it please the Court, I submit that there is no ground whatever to charge these defendants with any criminal offense.

1. Because the women who voted were legal voters.

2. Because they were challenged and took the oaths which the statute requires of Electors, and the Inspectors had no right, after such oath, to reject their votes.

1 R. S. Edmonds Ed., 126–127.

The duty of Inspectors of Election is defined by the Statute as follows:

"§ 13. If any person offering to vote at any election shall be challenged in relation to his right to vote at that election, by an Inspector, or by any other person entitled to vote at the same poll, one of the Inspectors shall tender to him the following preliminary oath: 'You do swear (or affirm) that you will truly and fully 'answer all such questions as shall be put to you 'touching your place of residence and qualifications 'as an Elector.'"

"§ 14. The Inspectors or one of them shall then proceed to question the person challenged in relation to his name; his then place of residence; how long he has resided in the town or ward where the vote is offered; what was the last place of his residence before he came into that town or ward, and also as to his citizenship, and whether a native or a naturalized citizen, and if the latter, when, where, and in what court, or before what officer, he was naturalized; whether he came into the town or ward for the purpose of voting at that election; how long he contemplates residing in the town or ward; and all such other questions as may tend to test his qualifications as a resident of the town or ward, citizenship and right to vote at that poll."

"§ 15. If any person shall refuse to take the said preliminary oath when so tendered, or to answer fully any questions which shall be so put to him, his vote shall be rejected."

"§ 16. After receiving the answers of the person so challenged, the board of inspectors shall point out to him the qualifications, if any, in respect to which he shall appear to them deficient."

"§ 17. If the person so offering shall persist in his claim to vote, and the challenge shall not be withdrawn, one of the inspectors shall then administer the following oath: 'You do swear (or affirm as the case may be) that you have been a citizen of the United States for ten days, and are now of the age of twenty one years; that you have been an inhabitant of this State for one year next preceding this election, and for the last four months a resident of this County; that you have been for thirty days next preceding this election a resident of this Assembly district (or Senate or Congressional district or districts, ward, town, village or city from which the officer is to be chosen for whom said person offers to vote); that you are now a resident of this town (or ward, as the case may be) and of the election district in which you now offer to vote, and that you have not made any bet or wager, and are not directly or indirectly interested in any bet or wager depending upon the result of this election, and that you have not voted at this election.'"

§ 18. Prescribes the form of oath to be administered to colored men.

"§ 19. If any person shall refuse to take the oath so tendered, his vote shall be rejected."

The defendants performed their duty strictly and fully according to the statute.

The persons offering to vote were challenged; the defendants administered the preliminary oath to them; all the questions required by the statute were answered fully and truly; the challenge was still insisted on; the general oath was administered by the defendants to them; they took that oath, and every word contained in it was true in their case. The inspectors had no alternative. They could not reject the votes.

This statute has been construed by the Court of Appeals of this State in the case of *The People vs. Pease*, 27 *N. Y.* 45.

In that case it is held, that inspectors of election have no authority by statute to reject a vote except in three cases: (1) after a refusal to take the preliminary oath, or (2) fully to answer any questions put, or (3) on refusal to take the general oath.

Davies J., in his opinion after an examination of the provisions of the statute says:

"*It is seen, therefore, that the inspectors have no authority,* "*by statute, to reject a vote except in the three cases: after* "*refusal to take the preliminary oath, or fully to answer any* "*questions put, or on refusal to take the general oath. And* "*the only judicial discretion vested in them is, to determine* "*whether any question put to the person offering to vote, has or* "*has not, been fully answered. If the questions put have been* "*fully answered, and such answers discover the fact, that* "*the person offering to vote is not a qualified voter, yet if* "*he persists in his claim to vote it is imperative upon the* "*inspectors to administer to him the general oath, and if taken,* "*to receive the vote and deposit the same in the ballot box.*"

Selden, J., who wrote in the same case, examines this question with great care and reaches the same conclusion. He says:

"The course required by the statute, to be pursued "where the right of any person to vote is challenged, "cannot be reconciled with any discretionary power of "rejection vested in the inspectors. (Citing the stat- "ute as above quoted.) The inspectors are, first, to "administer what is called the preliminary oath, re- "quiring the person offering the vote to answer such "questions as shall be put to him touching his place "of residence and qualifications as an elector. The "statute then mentions several questions which are "to be addressed to him by the inspectors, and au- "thorizes such other questions as may tend to test his "qualifications as a voter. If he refuse to take the "oath, or to answer fully, his vote is to be rejected; "but if he answers fully, the inspectors are required "to point out to him the qualifications, if any, in "which he shall appear to them to be deficient. If "he still persists in his right to vote, and the challenge "is not withdrawn, the inspectors are required to ad- "minister to him the general oath, in which he states "in detail, and swears, that he possesses all the qual- "ifications the Constitution and laws require the voter "to possess. *If he refuse to take the oath, his vote shall "be rejected.* Is not the inference irresistible, that, if "he take the oath, it shall be received? If his vote is "to be rejected after he takes the oath, why not reject "it before? *As I construe the statute, the inspectors have "no discretion left them in such a case* (where the person "offering to vote is not shown by a record to have been "convicted of a crime, or by his own oath to be inter- "ested in a bet upon the election,) *but must deposit the "ballot in the box, whatever they may believe or know of "the want of qualifications of the voter. They are re- "quired to act upon the evidence which the statute prescribes, "and have no judicial power to pass upon the question of "its truth or falsehood; nor can they act upon their own "opinion or knowledge.*"

These views were concurred in by all the Judges. *Denio*, J., who wrote a dissenting opinion in the case, concurred with the other Judges as to the powers and duties of inspectors.

The defendants, then, have not in the least violated any law of the State of New York. They performed their duty according to the statute and in accordance with the decision of the highest court of the State, and in accordance with the printed instructions furnished them by the Secretary of State. What further can be demanded of them? No United States statute prescribes or attempts to prescribe their duties. They cannot legally be convicted and should be discharged.

3. Because no malice is shown. Whether the women were entitled to have their names registered and to vote, or not, the defendants believed they had such right, and acted in good faith, according to their best judgment, in allowing the registry of their names—and in receiving their votes—and whether they decided right or wrong in point of law, they are not guilty of any criminal offense.

The substance of the statute is, as to registration:
"If any such officer shall *knowingly and wilfully* "register as a voter any person not entitled to be reg-"istered, or refuse to so register any person entitled to "be registered * * * * every such person shall "be deemed guilty of a crime."

Act of May 31, 1870, § 20, As Amended by Act of Feb. 28, 1871, § 1.

And as to voting:
"If any person shall * * * * *knowingly and* "*wilfully* receive the vote of any person not entitled "to vote, or refuse to receive the vote of any person "entitled to vote * * * * every such person "shall be deemed guilty of a crime."

Act of May 31, 1870, § 19.

To bring an inspector within either of these sections he must know as *matter of fact*, that the person offering to vote, or to be registered, is not entitled to be registered or to vote.

The inspectors were *compelled to decide the question*, and to decide it instantly, with no chance for examination or even consultation—and if they decided in good faith, according to the best of their ability, they are excused, whether they decided correctly or not in point of law.

This is too well settled to admit of dispute—settled by authority as well as by the plainest principles of justice and common sense.

The law never yet placed a public officer in a position where he would be compelled to decide a doubtful legal question, and to act upon his decision, *subject to the penalty of fine* or imprisonment if he chanced to err in his decision.

All that is ever required of an officer, so placed, whether a judicial or ministerial officer, *so far as is necessary to escape any imputations of crime*, is good faith.

Ministerial officers may be required, in some cases to act at their peril as to *civil* responsibilities, but as to *criminal responsibilities* never.

Inspectors of elections, however, *acting in good faith*, incur neither civil nor criminal responsibilities.

In *Jenkins vs. Waldron* (11 *John* 114), which was an action on the case against inspectors of election for refusing to receive the vote of the plaintiff, a duly qualified voter, it was held, that the action would not lie *without proving malice*. Spencer, J., delivering the opinion of the Court, closes as follows: "It would in "our opinion be opposed to all the principles of law, "justice and sound policy, to hold that officers called "upon to exercise their deliberate judgments, *are* "*answerable for a mistake in law*, either civilly or "criminally, where their motives are pure and un- "tainted with fraud or malice."

The same point precisely was decided in a like case, in the Supreme Court of this State recently and *Jenkins vs. Waldron approved.*

Goetchens vs. Mathewson, 5 Lansing, 214.

In Harman v. Tappenden and fifteen others (1 East 555) the plaintiff was a freeman of the company of free fishermen and dredgermen of the manor and hundred of Faversham in Kent, and the defendants, as officers of the company, caused him "wrongfully, unlawfully and unjustly" to be disfranchised, and removed from his said office of freeman. He was restored by mandamus, and brought his action on the case against the defendants who removed him, to recover his damages.

On the trial befor Lord Kenyon, C. J., a verdict was taken for the plaintiff for nominal damages, with leave to the defendant to move to enter a non-suit.

On that motion Lord Kenyon, C. J., said:

"Have you any precedent to show that an action of "this sort will lie, without proof of malice in the de- "fendants, or that the act of disfranchisement was "done on purpose to deprive the plaintiff of the par- "ticular advantage which resulted to him from his "corporate character? I believe this is a case of the "first impression, where an action of this kind had "been brought, *upon a mere mistake, or error in judg- "ment.* The plaintiff had broken a by-law, for which "he had incurred certain penalties, and happening to "be personally present in the court, he was called up- "on to show cause why he should not pay the forfeit- "ures; to which not making any answer, but refusing "to pay them, the court proceeded, taking the offense "*pro confesso,* without any proof, to call on him to "show cause why he should not be disfranchised; and "they accordingly made the order. This was undoubt-"edly irregular, but it was nothing more than a mis-"take, and there was no ground to impute any malicious "motives to the persons making the order."

Lawrence, J., said: "There is no instance of an "action of this sort maintained for an act merely from "error of judgment. Perhaps the action might have "been maintained, if it had been proved that the de-"fendants' contriving and intending to injure and "prejudice the plaintiff, and to deprive him of the "benefit of his profits from the fishery, which as a "member of this body he was entitled to, according to "the custom, had *wilfully and maliciously* procured "him to be disfranchised, in consequence of which he "was deprived of such profits. But here there was "no evidence of any wilful and malicious intention to "deprive the plaintiff of his profits, or that they had "disfranchised him with that intent, *which is neces-"sary to maintain this action.* They were indeed "guilty of an error in their proceedings to disfranchise "him, in not going into any proof of the offence charg-"ed against him, but taking his silence as a confes-"sion. In the case of *Drewe v. Coulton*, where the "action was against the Mayor of Saltash, who was "returning officer, for refusing the plaintiff's vote at "an election, which was claimed in right of a burgage "tenement; Wilson, J., nonsuited the plaintiff *because "malice was not proved;* and he observed, that "though Lord Holt, in the case of *Ashby v. White*, en-"deavored to show that the action lay for the ob-"struction of the right, yet the House of Lords, in "the justification of their conduct, supposed to be "written by the Chief Justice, puts it upon a different "principle, the *wilfulness of the act.* The declaration "in that case was copied from the precedent in *Mil-"ward v. Sargeant*, which came on in this court on a "writ of error, *Hill 26, Geo. 3*, for refusing the plain-"tiff's vote for the borough of Hastings. There the "charge was 'that the defendant contriving and wrong-"fully intending to injure and prejudice the plaintiff, "and to hinder and deprive him of his privilege of "voting, did not take or allow his vote.' All which "allegations Mr. Justice WILSON, in the case above "alluded to, thought were essential to be proved in "order to sustain the action."

"*Per Curiam.* Rule discharged."

The Reporter's head note is: "An action does not lie against individuals for acts erroneously done by them *in a corporate capacity* from which detriment has happened to the plaintiff. At least, not without proof of malice."

The case of *Drewe v. Coulton* is given at length in a note to *Harman v. Tappenden and others 1 East 563*, and fully sustains what is said of it by Mr. Justice Lawrence.

The election was for member to serve in Parliament for the borough of SALTASH. The defendant was Mayor and returning officer. The question presented to him was "whether the owners of burgage tenements in the borough, had a right of voting, or whether that right was confined to the freemen of the corporation." The defendant had rejected the vote offered by the plaintiff, he claiming the right as a burgage tenant.

The action was for that refusal, charging the defendant with "contriving and wrongfully intending to deprive the plaintiff &c., obstructed and hindered him from giving his vote."

Wilson, J., among other things, says: "This is in the nature of it, an action for misbehavior by a public officer in his duty. Now I think, that it cannot be called a misbehavior, *unless maliciously and wilfully done*, *and that the action will not lie for a mistake in law.* The case of the bridge master is in point [Bul N. P. 64.] It is there said, that an action on the case lies against a ministerial officer for *wilful* misbehavior, as denying a poll for one who is a candidate for an elective office, such as bridge master &c." "In all the cases put, the "misbehavior must be *wilful and by wilful* I understand *contrary to a man's own conviction.* Therefore I "think from the opening of counsel, this is not a wilful "refusal of the vote. * * * In very few "instances is an officer answerable for what he does to "the best of his judgment, in cases where he is compelled to act. But the action lies where the officer "has an option whether he will act or not. Besides, I "think, that if an action were to be brought upon "every occasion of this kind by every person whose "vote was refused, it would be such an inconvenience "as the law would not endure. A returning officer "in such a case would be in a most perilous situation. "*This gentleman was put in a situation where he was* "*bound to act; and if he acted to the best of his judgment* "*it would be a great hardship that he should be answerable* "*for the consequences, even though he is mistaken in a* "*point of law.* It was a very material observation of Mr. "Gibbs, that the words of the resolution of the *House of* "*Lords* in *Ashby v. White* followed the words of the statute of William III. For if that statute were declaratory of the common law, as it purports to be [Be it "enacted and declared that all false returns wilfully "made' &c.] and an action would not lie at common "law for a false return, unless the return be proved "to have been made maliciously, as well as falsely, it "should seem, by a parity of reasoning, that a person "whose vote is refused by a returning officer, cannot "maintain an action against him, unless the refusal *be* "*proved to have been wilful and malicious.* And if "malice were necessary before the statute by the common law, and since by the statute which is declaratory thereof, to sustain an action for a false return "which includes perhaps the votes of all, it seems "equally necessary in an action like the present where "the injury complained of is to one only.

"I do not mean to say, that in this kind of action, "it is necessary to prove *express* malice. It is sufficient "cient if malice may be implied from the conduct of "the officer; as if he had decided contrary to a last "resolution of the House of Commons. There *I should* "*leave it to the jury to imply malice.* But taking all "*the circumstances of this case together, malice can in* "*no shape be imputed to the defendant. The plaintiff* "*may have a right to vote, but that depends upon an intri*-"*cate question of law, with respect to burgage tenures*; the "the right itself founded on ancient documents and "usages, and not acted upon for many years. * *

"*From these grounds, therefore, it cannot be infer*-"*red that the defendant has acted wilfully and ma*-"*liciously in refusing the plaintiff's vote; and* "*unless that be so he is not liable in this action.*

* * * "But without determining whether "the statute be declaratory of the common law, or not; "if not, the case rests on that of *Ashby v. White.* "Now all the debates and arguments in that case *go* "*upon the malice*; and all those who have acted on "that determination since have considered that the "refusal must be *wilful and malicious* in order to "support the action. * * * * *

"And in my opinion, it cannot be said, that because "an officer is mistaken in a point of law, this action "will lie against him. * * It has also been "said, that this is not like a case where a burdensome "office is thrown upon a man, without his consent, "wherein he is compellable to act; for that here the "defendant has chosen to become a member of a cor-"poration by which he had put himself in a situation "to become a returning officer, and therefore that he is "*bound to understand the whole law as far as it* "*relates to his public situation, and is answerable for* "*any determination he may make contrary to that* "*law. But I much doubt whether that rule be gene-* "*rally true;* and in the present instance I am clearly " of opinion that the want of malice is a full defense."

Lawrence, J., sat with Wilson.

The plaintiff was nonsuited and no new trial was moved for.

Bernardiston v. Some (2 Lev. 114, 1 East. 586, note b.) was an action against the sheriff of Suffolk, charging that the defendant, intending to deprive him of the office of Knight of the Shire, made a double return. Upon a trial at bar, Twysden, Rainsford, and Wylie 'Js. held, and so directed the jury, that if the return was made *maliciously*, they ought to find for the plaintiff, which they did and gave him £800. On motion in arrest of judgment, Hale, C. J., being in court; he, Twysden & Wylie, Js. held that for as much as the return was laid to be *falso et malitiose et ea intentione*, to put the plaintiff to charge and expense, and so found by the jury, the action lay. Rainsford, J., doubted. But notwithstanding this charge of malice, judgment was reversed *in Cam scacc* (*vide 3 Lev. 30*) and that judgment of reversal was affirmed in Parliament. Lord Chief justice North's first reason against the action was, because the sheriff as to declaring the Mayoralty is *judge* and no action will lie against a judge for what he does judicially, though it should be laid *falso malitiose et scienter.* This reversal occasioned the passage of the statute (7 and 8 W. III c. 7) which gives an action against the returning officer, for all false returns "wilfully made, and for double returns *falsely, wilfully and maliciously made.*"

Groenvelt v. Burwell & al (1 Salk. 396, S. C. 2 Ld Ray. 230, Comyns 76.) In this case, the Censors of the College of Physicians and Surgeons, in London, were empowered to inspect, govern and censure, all practices of physic in London—and to punish by fine and imprisonment. They convicted the plaintiff of administering noxious medicines, and fined him £20, and imprisonment 12 months. Being taken in execution, he brought trespass against the Censors. It was held

1. That the Censors had judicial power.

2. That being judges of the the matter, what they had adjudged was not traversable. That the plaintiff could not be permitted to gainsay, what the Censors had said by their judgment—that the medicines were noxious.

3. Though the medicines were really good, yet no action lies against the Censors, because it is a wrong judgment in a matter within the limits of their jurisdiction; and a judge is not answerable, either to the King or the party, for the mistakes or errors of his judgment in a matter of which he has jurisdiction; It would expose the justice of the nation, and *no man would execute the office upon peril of being arraigned by action or indictment for every judgment he pronounces.*"

All that I have quoted from the English cases and our own to show that *malice* must be proven to make out the offense, *is expressly contained in the* statute under which this indictment is framed. The words are (Sec. 19) "shall knowingly and *wilfully* receive the vote of any person not entitled to vote." (And Section 20 as amended) "If any such officer shall knowingly and *wilfully* register, as a voter any person not entitled to vote."

And wilfully means, to use the language of Mr. Justice Wilson, "*contrary to a man's own conviction.*"

If it be said that the defendants must be presumed to know the law, that is answered above by the quotations from the opinion of Mr. Justice Wilson.

Besides when the statute speaks of "knowledge," aside from the expression "wilfully" it means *knowledge* as a *fact*—not any *forced presumption of knowledge* against the clear facts of the case.

To this extent and *to this extent only*, does the presumption that defendants were bound to know the law go, viz: They were bound to know that if they *as a fact* "knowingly and wilfully registered as a voter any person not entitled to be registered" or "knowingly and wilfully received the vote of any person not entitled to vote," in either case they were liable to the penalty; and they could not be allowed to urge in their defense any ignorance that *the law made those facts criminal.*

Here is a total absence of any pretence of malice. The defendants acted honestly and according to their best judgment. This is conceded. The most that can be said against them is, that they have erred in judgment. They are not lawyers, nor skilled in the law. They had presented to them a legal question which, to say the least, has puzzled some of the ablest legal minds of the nation. The penalty is the same, on which ever side they err. If they can be convicted of crime, a test must be imposed upon them, which no judge in the land could stand.

The defendants should be discharged by this Court.

Mr. Crowley then rose to make his argument, when the Court said:

THE COURT: I don't think it is necessary for you to spend time in argument, Mr. Crowley. I think upon the last authority cited by the counsel there is no defense in this case. It is entirely clear that where there is a distinct judicial act, the party performing the judicial act is not responsible, civilly or criminally, unless corruption is proven, and in many cases not when corruption is proven. But where the act is not judicial in its character—where there is no discretion—then there is no legal protection. That is the law, as laid down in the authority last quoted, and the authority quoted by Judge Selden in his opinion. It is undoubtedly good law. They hold expressly in that case that the inspectors are administrative officers, and not judicial officers.

Now, this is the point in the case, in my view of it: If there was any case in which a female was entitled to vote, then it would be a subject of examination. If a female over the age of 21 was entitled to vote, then it would be within the judicial authority of the inspectors to examine and determine whether in the given case the female came within that provision. If a married woman was entitled to vote, or if a married woman was not entitled to vote, and a single woman was entitled to vote, I think the inspectors would have a right in a case before them, to judge upon the evidence whether the person before them was married or single. If they decided erroneously, ther judicial character would protect them. But under the law of this state, as it stands, under no circumstances is a woman entitled to vote. When Miss Anthony, Mrs. Leyden and the other ladies came there and presented themselves for registry, and presented themselves to offer their votes, when it appeared that they were women—that they were of the female sex—the power and authority of the inspectors was at an end. When they act upon a subject upon which they have no discretion, I think there is no judicial authority. There is a large range of discretion in regard to the votes offered by the male sex. If a man offers his vote, there is a question whether he is a minor—whether he is 21 years of age. The subject is within their jurisdiction. If they decide correctly, it is well; if they decide erroneously, they act judicially, and are not liable. If the question is whether the person presenting his vote is a foreigner or naturalized, or whether he has been a resident of the state or district for a sufficient length of time, the subject is all within their jurisdiction, and they have a right to decide, and are protected if they decide wrong.

But upon the view which has been taken of this question of the right of females to vote, by the United States Court at Washington, and by the adjudication which was made this morning, upon this subject there is no discretion, and therefore I must hold that it affords no protection.

In that view of the case, is there anything to go to the jury?

Mr. Van Voorhis: Yes, your Honor.

The Court: What?

Mr. Van Voorhis: The jury must pass upon the whole case, and particularly as to whether any ballots were received for representative in Congress, or candidates for representative in Congress, and whether the defendants acted wilfully and maliciously.

The Court: It is too plain to argue that.

Mr. Van Voorhis: There is nothing but circumstantial evidence.

The Court: Your own witness testified to it.

Mr. Van Voorhis: But "knowingly," your Honor, implies knowing that it is a vote for representative in Congress.

The Court: That comes within the decision of the question of law. I don't see that there is anything to go to the jury.

Mr. Van Voorhis: I cannot take your Honor's view of the case, but of course must submit to it. We ask to go to the jury upon this whole case, and claim that in this case, as in all criminal cases, the right of trial by jury is made inviolate by the constitution—that the Court has no power to take it from the jury.

THE COURT: I am going to submit it to the jury.

Gentlemen of the Jury:

This case is now before you upon the evidence as it stands, and I shall leave the case with you to decide—

MR. VAN VOORHIS: I claim the right to address the jury.

THE COURT: I don't think there is anything upon which you can legitimately address the jury.

Gentlemen, the defendants are charged with knowingly, willfully and wrongfully receiving the votes of the ladies whose names are mentioned, in November last, in the City of Rochester. They are charged in the same indictment with willfully and improperly registering those ladies. I decided in the case this morning, which many of you heard, probably, that under the law as it stands the ladies who offered their votes had no right to vote whatever. I repeat that decision, and I charge you that they had no right to offer their votes. They having no right to offer their votes, the inspectors of election ought not to receive them. The additional question exists in this case whether the fact that they acted as inspectors will relieve them from the charge in this case. You have heard the views which I have given upon that. I think they are administrative officers. I charge you that they are administrative and ministerial officers in this respect, that they are not judicial officers whose action protects them, and that therefore they are liable in this case. But, instead of doing as I did in the case this morning—directing a verdict—I submit the case to you with these instructions, and you can decide it here, or you may go out.

MR. VAN VOORHIS; I ask your Honor to instruct the jury that if they find these inspectors acted honestly, in accordance with their best judgment, they should be acquitted.

The Court: I have expressly ruled to the contrary of that, gentlemen; that that makes no difference.

Mr. Van Voorhis: And that in this country—under the laws of this country—

The Court: That is enough—you need not argue it, Mr. Van Voorhis.

Mr. Van Voorhis: Then I ask your Honor to charge the jury that they must find the fact that these inspectors received the votes of these persons knowingly, and that such votes were votes for some person for member of Congress, there being in the case no evidence that any man was voted for, for member of Congress, and there being no evidence except that secret ballots were received; that the jury have a right to find for the defendants, if they choose.

The Court: I charge the jury that there is sufficient evidence to sustain the indictment, upon this point.

Mr. Van Voorhis: I ask your Honor also to charge the jury that there is sufficient evidence to sustain a verdict of not guilty.

The Court: I cannot charge that.

Mr. Van Voorhis: Then why should it go to the jury?

The Court: As a matter of form.

Mr. Van Voorhis: If the jury should find a verdict of not guilty, could your Honor set it aside?

The Court: I will debate that with you when the occasion arises.

Gentlemen, you may deliberate here, or retire, as you choose.

10

The jury retired for consultation, and the Court took a recess until 7 P. M.

The Court re-convened at 7 o'clock, when the clerk called the jury, and asked them if they had agreed upon their verdict.

The foreman replied in the negative, whereupon the Court said :

THE COURT : Is there anything upon which I can give you any advice, gentlemen, or any information ?

A JUROR : We stand 11 for conviction, and 1 opposed.

THE COURT : If that gentleman desires to ask any questions in respect to the questions of law, or the facts in the case, I will give him any information he desires. (No response from the jury.) It is quite proper, if any gentleman has any doubt about anything, either as to the law or the facts, that he should state it to the Court. Counsel are both present, and I can give such information as is correct.

A JUROR : I don't wish to ask any questions.

THE COURT : Then you may retire again, gentlemen. The Court will adjourn until to-morrow morning.

The jury retired, and after an absence of about ten minutes returned into court.

The clerk called the names of the jury and then said :

THE CLERK : Gentlemen, have you agreed upon your verdict ?

THE FOREMAN : We have.

THE CLERK : How say you, do you find the prisoners at the bar guilty of the offense whereof they stand indicted, or not guilty ?

THE FOREMAN: Guilty.

THE CLERK: Hearken to your verdict as it stands recorded by the Court. You say you find the prisoners at the bar guilty of the offense whereof they stand indicted, and so say you all.

MR. VAN VOORHIS: I ask that the jury be polled.

The clerk polled the jury, each juror answering in the affirmative to the question, "Is this your verdict?"

On the next day, June 19, 1873, the counsel for the defendants, Mr. John Van Voorhis, made a motion to the Court, for a new trial in behalf of Beverly W. Jones, Edwin T. Marsh and William B. Hall. The argument was oral and is not given, but the following are the grounds of the motion:

1. The indictment contains no sufficient statement of any crime under the Acts of Congress, upon which it is framed.

2. The Court has no jurisdiction of the subject matter of the offense.

3. It was an error, for which a new trial should be granted, to refuse the defendants the fundamental right to address the jury, through their counsel. This is a right guaranteed by the United States Constitution. (*See Article VI. of the amendments to the U. S. Constitution. 1 Graham & Waterman on New Trials, pages 682, 683 and 684.*)

4. The defendants were substantially deprived of the right of jury trial. The instructions of the Court to the jury were imperative. They were equivalent to a direction to find a verdict of guilty. It was said by the Court in the hearing of the jury, that the case was submitted to the jury "as a matter of form." The jury was not at liberty to exercise its own judgment upon

the evidence, and without committing a gross discourtesy to the Court, could render no verdict except that of guilty.

5. Admitting that the defendants acted without malice, or any corrupt motive, and in accordance with their best judgments, and in perfect good faith, it was error to charge that that was no defense.

6. The defendants are admitted to have acted in accordance with their duty as defined by the laws of New York (*1 R. S., Edmond's Ed., pp. 126–127, sections 13, 14, 15, 16, 17, 18 and 19*) as construed by the Court of Appeals. (*People vs. Pease, 27 N. Y. 45.*)

They are administrative officers and bound to regard only the evidence which the Statute prescribes. They are not clothed with the power, to reject the vote of a person who has furnished the evidence, which the law requires, of right to vote, on what they or either of them might know, as to the truth or falsity of such evidences. They have no discretion, and must perform their duty, as it is defined by the laws of New York and the decisions of her Courts.

7. The defendant, William B. Hall, has been tried and convicted in his absence from the Court. This is an error fatal to the conviction in his case.

The Court denied the motion.

The Court then asked the defendants if they had anything to say why sentence should not be pronounced, in response to which Beverly W. Jones said:

"Your honor has pronounced me guilty of crime; "the jury had but little to do with it. In the perform-"ance of my duties as an inspector of election, which "position I have held for the last four years, I acted con-"scientiously, faithfully and according to the best of "my judgment and ability. I did not believe that I "had a right to reject the ballot of a citizen who of "fered to vote, and who took the preliminary and gene- "ral oaths; and answered all questions prescribed by "law. The instructions furnished me by the State "authorities declared that I had no such right. As far "as the registry of the names is concerned, they would "never have been placed upon the registry, if it had "not been for Daniel Warner, the Democratic federal "Supervisor of elections, appointed by this Court, who "not only advised the registry, but addressed us, saying, "'Young men, do you know the penalty of the law if you "refuse to register these names?' And after discharg- "ing my duties faithfully and honestly and to the best "of my ability, if it is to vindicate the law that I am "to be imprisoned, I willingly submit to the penalty."

And Edwin T. Marsh said:

"In October last, just previous to the time fixed for "the sitting of the Board of Registrars in the first dis- "trict of the eighth ward of Rochester, a vacancy oc- "curred. I was solicited to act, and consenting, was "duly appointed by the Common council.

"I had never given the matter a thought until called "to the position, and as a consequence knew nothing "of the law. On the morning of the first day of the "last session of the Board, Miss Anthony and other "women presented themselves and claimed the right "to be registered. So far as I knew, the question of "woman suffrage had never come up in that shape be- "fore. We were in a position where we could take no "middle course.

"Decide which way we might, we were liable to "prosecution. We devoted all the time to acquiring "information on the subject, that our duties as Regis- "trars would allow.

"We were expected, it seems, to make an infallible "decision, inside of two days, of a question in regard "to which some of the best minds of the country are "divided. The influences by which we were surround- "ed, were nearly all in unison with the course we took. "I believed then, and believe now, that we acted *law- "fully.*

"I faithfully discharged the duties of my office, ac- "cording to the best of my ability, in strict compliance "with the oath administered to me. I consider the "argument of our counsel unanswered and unanswer- "able."

" *The verdict is not the verdict of the jury.*

"*I am* NOT GUILTY *of the charge.*"

The Court then sentenced the defendants to pay a fine of $25 each, and the costs of the prosecution.

APPENDIX.

ADDRESS OF

SUSAN B. ANTHONY,

Delivered in twenty-nine of the Post Office Districts of Monroe, and twenty-one of Ontario, in her canvass of those Counties, prior to her trial in June, 1873.

Friends and Fellow-citizens: I stand before you to-night, under indictment for the alleged crime of having voted at the last Presidential election, without having a lawful right to vote. It shall be my work this evening to prove to you that in thus voting, I not only committed no crime, but, instead, simply exercised my *citizen's right,* guaranteed to me and all United States citizens by the National Constitution, beyond the power of any State to deny.

Our democratic-republican government is based on the idea of the natural right of every individual member thereof to a voice and a vote in making and executing the laws. We assert the province of government to be to secure the people in the enjoyment of their unalienable rights. We throw to the winds the old dogma that governments can give rights. Before governments were organized, no one denies that each individual possessed the right to protect his own life, liberty and property. And when 100 or 1,000,000 people enter into a free government, they do not barter away their natural rights; they simply pledge themselves to protect each other in the enjoyment of them, through prescribed judicial and legislative tribunals. They agree to abandon the methods of brute force in the adjustment of their differences, and adopt those of civilization.

Nor can you find a word in any of the grand documents left us by the fathers that assumes for government the power to create or to confer rights. The Declaration of Independence, the United States Constitution, the constitutions of the several states and the organic laws of the territories, all alike propose to protect the people in the exercise of their God-given rights. Not one of them pretends to bestow rights.

"All men are created equal, and endowed by their Creator with certain unalienable rights. Among these are life, liberty and the pursuit of happiness. That to secure these, governments are instituted among men, deriving their just powers from the consent of the governed."

Here is no shadow of government authority over rights, nor exclusion of any class from their full and equal enjoyment. Here is pronounced the right of all men, and "consequently," as the Quaker preacher said, "of all women," to a voice in the government. And here, in this very first paragraph of the declaration, is the assertion of the natural right of all to the ballot; for, how can "the consent of the governed" be given, if the right to vote be denied. Again:

"That whenever any form of government becomes destructive of these ends, it is the right of the people to alter or abolish it, and to institute a new government, laying its foundations on such principles, and organizing its powers in such forms as to them shall seem most likely to effect their safety and happiness."

Surely, the right of the whole people to vote is here clearly implied. For however destructive to their happiness this government might become, a disfranchised class could neither alter nor abolish it, nor institute a new one, except by the old brute force method of insurrection and rebellion. One-half of the people of this nation to-day are utterly powerless to blot from the statute books an unjust law, or to write there a new and a just one. The women, dissatisfied as they are with this form of government, that enforces taxation without representation,—that compels them to obey laws to which they have never given their consent,—that imprisons and hangs them without a trial by a jury of their peers, that robs them, in marriage, of the custody of their own persons, wages and children,—are this half of the people left wholly at the mercy of the other half, in direct violation of the spirit and letter of the declarations of the framers of this government, every one of which was based on the immutable principle of equal rights to all. By those declarations, kings, priests, popes, aristocrats, were all alike dethroned, and placed on a common level, politically, with the lowliest born subject or serf. By them, too, men, as such, were deprived of their divine right to rule, and placed on a political level with women. By the practice of those declarations all class and caste distinction will be abolished; and slave, serf, plebeian, wife, woman, all alike, bound from their subject position to the proud platform of equality.

The preamble of the federal constitution says:

"We, the people of the United States, in order to form a more perfect union, establish justice, insure *domestic* tranquility, provide for the common defence, promote the general welfare and secure the blessings of liberty to ourselves and our posterity, do ordain and establish this constitution for the United States of America."

It was we, the people, not we, the white male citizens, nor yet we, the male citizens; but we, the whole people, who formed this Union. And we formed it, not to give the blessings of liberty, but to securc them; not to the half of ourselves and the half of our posterity, but to the whole people—women as well as men. And it is downright mockery to talk to women of their enjoyment of the blessings of liberty while they are denied the use of the only means of securing them provided by this democratic-republican government—the ballot.

The early journals of Congress show that when the committee reported to that body the original articles of confederation, the very first article which became the subject of discussion was that respecting equality of suffrage. Article 4th said:

"The better to secure and perpetuate mutual friendship and intercourse between the people of the different States of this Union, the free inhabitants of each of the States, (paupers, vagabonds and fugitives from justice excepted,) shall be entitled to all the privileges and immunities of the free citizens of the several States."

Thus, at the very beginning, did the fathers see the necessity of the universal application of the great principle of equal rights to all—in order to produce the desired result—a harmonious union and a homogeneous people.

Luther Martin, attorney-general of Maryland, in his report to the Legislature of that State of the convention that framed the United States Constitution, said:

"Those who advocated the equality of suffrage took the matter up on the origiaal principles of government: that the reason why each individual man in forming a State government should have an equal vote, is because each individual, before he enters into government, is equally free and equally independent."

James Madison said;

"Under every view of the subject, it seems indispensable that the mass of the citizens should not be without a voice in making the laws which they are to obey, and in choosing the magistrates who are to administer them." Also, "Let it be remembered, finally, that it has ever been the pride and the boast of America that the rights for which she contended were the rights of human nature."

And these assertions of the framers of the United States Constitution of the equal and natural rights of all the people to a voice in the government, have been affirmed and reaffirmed by the leading statesmen of the nation, throughout the entire history of our government.

Thaddeus Stevens, of Pennsylvania, said in 1866:

"I have made up my mind that the elective franchise is one of the inalienable rights meant to be secured by the declaration of independence."

B. Gratz Brown, of Missouri, in the three days' discussion in the United States Senate in 1866, on Senator Cowan's motion to strike "male" from the District of Columbia suffrage bill, said:

"Mr. President, I say here on the floor of the American Senate, I stand for universal suffrage; and as a matter of fundamental principle, do not recognize the right of society to limit it on any ground of race or sex. I will go farther and say, that I recognize the right of franchise as being intrinsically a natural right. I do not believe that society is authorized to impose any limitations upon it that do not spring out of the necessities of the social state itself. Sir, I have been shocked, in the course of this debate, to hear Senators declare this right only a conventional and political arrangement, a privilege yielded to you and me and others; not a right in any sense, only a concession! Mr. President, I do not hold my liberties by any such tenure. On the contrary, I believe that whenever you establish that doctrine, whenever you crystalize that idea in the public mind of this country, you ring the death-knell of American liberties."

Charles Sumner, in his brave protests against the fourteenth and fifteenth amendments, insisted that, so soon as by the thirteenth amendment the slaves became free men, the original powers of the United States Constitution guaranteed to them equal rights—the right to vote and to be voted for. In closing one of his great speeches he said;

"I do not hesitate to say that when the slaves of our country became 'citizens' they took their place in the body politic as a component part of the 'people,' entitled to equal rights, and under the protection of these two guardian principles: First—That all just governments stand on the consent of the governed; and second, that taxation without representation is tyranny; and these rights it is the duty of Congress to guarantee as essential to the idea of a Republic."

The preamble of the Constitution of the State of New York declares the same pnrpose. It says:

"We, the people of the State of New York, grateful to Almighty God for our freedom, in order to secure its blessings, do establish this Constitution."

Here is not the slightest intimation, either of receiving freedom from the United States Constitution, or of the State conferring the blessings of liberty upon the people; and the same is true of every one of the thirty-six State Constitutions. Each and all, alike declare rights God-given, and that to secure the people in the enjoyment of their inalienable rights, is their one and only object in ordaining and establishing government. And all of the State Constitutions are equally emphatic in their recognition of the ballot as the means of securing the people in the enjoyment of these rights.

Article 1 of the New York State Constitution says:

"No member of this State shall be disfranchised or deprived of the rights or privileges secured to any citizen thereof, unless by the law of the land, or the judgment of his peers."

And so carefully guarded is the citizen's right to vote, that the Constitution makes special mention of all who may be excluded. It says:

"Laws may be passed excluding from the right of suffrage all persons who have been or may be convicted of bribery, larceny or any infamous crime."

In naming the various employments that shall not affect the residence of voters—the 3d section of article 2d says "that being kept at any alms house, or other asylum, at public expense, nor being confined at any public prison, shall deprive a person of his residence," and hence his vote. Thus is the right of voting most sacredly hedged about. The only seeming permission in the New York State Constitution for the disfranchisement of women is in section 1st of article 2d, which says:

"Every male citizen of the age of twenty-one years, &c., shall be entitled to vote."

But I submit that in view of the explicit assertions of the equal right of the whole people, both in the preamble and previous article cf the constitution, this omission of the adjective "female" in the second, should not be construed into a denial; but, instead, counted as of no effect. Mark the direct prohibition: "No member of this State shall be disfranchised, unless by the 'law of the land,' or the judgment of his peers." "The law of the land," is the United States Constitution: and there is no provision in that document that can be fairly construed into a permission to the States to deprive any class of their citizens of their right to vote. Hence New York can get no power from that source to disfranchise one entire half of her members. Nor has "the judgment of their peers" been pronounced against women exercising their right to vote; no disfranchised person is allowed to be judge or juror—and none but disfranchised persons can be women's peers; nor has the legislature passed laws excluding them on account of idiocy or lunacy; nor yet the courts convicted them of bribery, larceny, or any infamous crime. Clearly, then, there is no constitutional ground for the exclusion of women from the ballot-box in the State of New York, No barriers whatever stand to-day between women and the exercise of their right to vote save those of precedent and prejudice.

The clauses of the United States Constitution, cited by our opponents as giving power to the States to disfranchise any classes of citizens they shall please, are contained in sections 2d and 4th of article 1st. The second says:

"The House of Representatives shall be composed of members chosen every second year by the people of the several States; and the electors in each State shall have the qualifications requisite for electors of the most numerous branch of the State Leigslature."

This cannot be construed into a concession to the States of the power to destroy the right to become an elector, but simply to prescribe what shall be the qualifications, such as competency of intellect, maturity of age, length of residence, that shall be deemed necessary to enable them to make an intelligent choice of candidates. If, as our opponents assert, the last claause of this section makes it the duty of the United States to protect citizens in the several States against higher or different qualifications for electors for representatives in Congress, than for members of Assembly, then must the first clause make it equally imperative for the national government to interfere with the States, and forbid them from arbitrarily cutting off the right of one-half of the people to become electors altogether. Section 4th says:

"The times, places and manner of holding elections for Senators and Representatives shall be prescribed in each State by the Legislature thereof; but Congress may at any time, by law, make or alter such regulations, except as to the places of choosing Senators."

Here is conceded the power only to prescribe times, places and manner of holding the elections; and even with these Congress may interfere, with all excepting the mere place of choosing Senators. Thus you see, there is not the slightest permission in either section for the States to discriminate against the right of any class of citizens to vote. Surely, to regulate cannot be to annihilate! nor to qualify to wholly deprive. And to this principle every true Democrat and Republican said amen, when applied to black men by Senator Sumner in his great speeches for EQUAL RIGHTS TO ALL from 1865 to 1869; and when, in 1871, I asked that Senator to declare the power of the United States Constitution to protect women in their right to vote—as he had done for black men—he handed me a copy of all his speeches during that reconstruction period, and said:

"Miss Anthony, put 'sex' where I have 'race' or 'color,' and you have here the best and strongest argument I can make for woman. There is not a doubt but women have the constitutional right to vote, and I will never vote for a sixteenth amendment to guarantee it to them. I voted for both the fourteenth and fifteenth under protest; would never have done it but for the pressing emergency of that hour; would have insisted that the power of the original Constitution to protect all citizens in the equal enjoyment of their rights should have been vindicated through the courts. But the newly made freedmen had neither the intelligence, wealth nor time to wait that slow process. Women possess all these in an eminent degree, and I insist that they shall appeal to the courts, and through them establish the powers of our American *magna charta*, to protect every citizen of the Republic. But, friends, when in accordance with Senator Sumner's counsel, I went to the ballot-box, last November, and exercised my citizen's right to vote, the courts did not wait for me to appeal to them—they appealed to me, and indicted me on the charge of having voted illegally.

Senator Sumner, putting sex where he did color, said:

"Qualifications cannot be in their nature permanent or insurmountable. Sex cannot be a qualification any more than size, race, color, or previous condition of servitude. A permanent or insurmountable qualification is equivalent to a deprivation of the suffrage. In other words, it is the tyranny of taxation without representation, against which our revolutionary mothers, as well as fathers, rebelled."

For any State to make sex a qualification that must ever result in the disfranchisement of one entire half of the people, is to pass a bill of attainder, or an *ex post facto* law, and is therefore a violation of the supreme law of the land. By it, the blessings of liberty are forever withheld from women and their female posterity. To them, this government has no just powers derived from the consent of the governed. To them this government is not a democracy. It is not a republic. It is an odious aristocracy; a hateful obligarchy of sex. The most hateful aristocracy ever established on the face of the globe. An obligarchy of wealth, where the rich govern the poor; an obligarchy of learning, where the educated govern the ignorant; or even an obligarchy of race, where the Saxon rules the African, might be endured; but this obligarchy of sex, whieh makes father, brothers, husband, sons, the obligarchs over the mother and sisters, the wife and daughters of every household; which ordains all men sovereigns, all women subjects, carries dissension, discord and rebellion into every home of the nation. And this most odious aristocracy exists, too, in the face of Section 4, of Article 4, which says:

"The United States shall guarantee to every State in the Union a republican form of government."

What, I ask you, is the distinctive difference between the inhabitants of a monarchical and those of a republican form of government, save that in the monarchical the people are subjects, helpless, powerless, bound to obey laws made by superiors—while in the republican, the people are citizens, individual sovereigns, all clothed with equal power, to make and unmake both their laws and law makers, and the moment you deprive a person of his right to a voice in the government, you degrade him from the status of a citizen of the republic, to that of a subject, and it matters very little to him whether his monarch be an individual tyrant, as is the Czar of Russia, or a 15,000,000 headed monster, as here in the United States; he is a powerless subject, serf or slave; not a free and independent citizen in any sense.

But, it is urged, the use of the masculine pronouns he, his and him, in all the constitutions and laws, is proof that only men were meant to be included in their provisions. If you insist on this version of the letter of the law, we shall insist that you be consistent, and accept the other horn of the dilemna, which would compel you to exempt women from taxation for the support of the government, and from penalties for the violation of laws.

A year and a half ago I was at Walla Walla, Washington Territory. I saw there a theatrical company, called the "Pixley Sisters," playing before crowded houses, every night of the whole week of the territorial fair. The eldest of those three fatherless girls was scarce eighteen. Yet every night a United States officer stretched out his long fingers, and clutched six dollars of the proceeds of the exhibitions of those orphan girls, who, but a few years before, were half starvelings in the streets of Olympia, the capital of that far-off north-west territory. So the poor widow, who keeps a boarding house, manufactures shirts, or sells apples and peanuts on the street corners of our cities, is compelled to pay taxes from her scanty pittance. I would that the women of this republic, at once, resolve, never again to submit to taxation, until their right to vote be recognized.

Miss Sarah E. Wall, of Worcester, Mass., twenty years ago, took this position. For several years, the officers of the law distrained her property, and sold it to meet the necessary amount; still she persisted, and would not yield an iota, though every foot of her lands should be struck off under the hammer. And now, for several years, the assessor has left her name off the tax list, and the collector passed her by without a call.

Mrs. J. S. Weeden, of Viroqua, Wis., for the past six years, has refused to pay her taxes, though the annual assessment is $75.

Mrs. Ellen Van Valkenburg, of Santa Cruz, Cal., who sued the County Clerk for refusing to register her name, declares she will never pay another dollar of tax until allowed to vote; and all over the country, women property holders are waking up to the injustice of taxation without representation, and ere long will refuse, *en masse,* to submit to the imposition.

There is no she, or her, or hers, in the tax laws.

The statute of New York reads:

"Every person shall be assessed in the town or ward where *he* resides when the assessment is made, for the lands owned by *him,* &c." "Every collector shall call at least once on the person taxed, or at *his* usual place of residence, and shall demand payment of the taxes charged on *him.* If any one shall refues to pay the tax imposed on *him,* the collector shall levy the same by distress and sale of *his* property."

The same is true of all the criminal laws:

"No person shall be compelled to be a witness against *himself,* &c."

The same with the law of May 31st, 1870, the 19th section of which I am charged with having violated; not only are all the pronouns in it masculine, but everybody knows that that particular section was intended expressly to hinder the rebels from voting. It reads "If any person shall knowingly vote without *his* having a lawful right," &c. Precisely so with all the papers served on me—the U. S. Marshal's warrant, the bail-bond, the petition for habeas corpus, the bill of indictment—not one of them had a feminine pronoun printed in it; but, to make them applicable to me, the Clerk of the Court made a little carat at the left of "he" and placed an "s" over it, thus making *she* out of *he*. Then the letters "is" were scratched out, the little carat under and "er" over, to make *her* out of *his*, and I insist if government officials may thus manipulate the pronouns to tax, fine, imprison and hang women, women may take the same liberty with them to secure to themselves their right to a voice in the government.

So long as any classes of men were denied their right to vote, the government made a show of consistency, by exempting them from taxation. When a property qualification of $250 was required of black men in New York, they were not compelled to pay taxes, so long as they were content to report themselves worth less than that sum; but the moment the black man died, and his property fell to his widow or daughter, the black woman's name would be put on the assessor's list, and she be compelled to pay taxes on the same property exempted to her husband. The same is true of ministers in New York. So long as the minister lives, he is exempted from taxation on $1,500 of property, but the moment the breath goes out of his body, his widow's name will go down on the assessor's list, and she will have to pay taxes on the $1,500. So much for the special legislation in favor of women.

In all the penalties and burdens of the government, (except the military,) women are reckoned as citizens, equally with men. Also, in all the privileges and immunities, save those of the jury box and ballot box, the two fundamental privileges on which rest all the others. The United States government not only taxes, fines, imprisons and hangs women, but it allows them to pre-empt lands, register ships, and take out passport and naturalization papers. Not only does the law permit single women and widows to the right of naturalization, but Section 2 says: "A married woman may be naturalized without the concurrence of her husband." (I wonder the fathers were not afraid of creating discord in the families of foreigners); and again: "When an alien, having complied with the law, and declared his intention to become a citizen, dies before he is actually naturalized, his widow and children shall be considered citizens, entitled to all rights and privileges as such, on taking the required oath." If a foreign born woman by becoming a naturalized citizen, is entitled to all the rights and privileges of citizenship, is not a native born woman, by her national citizenship, possessed of equal rights and privileges?

The question of the masculine pronouns, yes and nouns, too, has been settled by the United States Supreme Court, in the Case of *Silver versus Ladd*, December, 1868, in a decision as to whether a woman was entitled to lands, under the Oregon donation law of 1850. Elizabeth Cruthers, a widow, settled upon a claim, and received patents. She died, and her son was heir. He died. Then Messrs. Ladd & Nott took possession, under the general pre-emption law, December, 1861. The administrator, E. P. Silver, applied for a writ of ejectment at the land office in Oregon City. Both the Register and Receiver decided that an unmarried woman could not hold land under that law. The Commissioner of the General Land Office, at Washington, and the Secretary of the Interior, also gave adverse opinions. Here patents were issued to Ladd & Nott, and duly recorded. Then a suit was brought to set aside Ladd's patent, and it was carried through all the State Courts and the Supreme Court of Oregon, each, in turn, giving adverse decisions. At last, in the United States Supreme Court, Associate Justice Miller reversed the decisions of all the lower tribunals, and ordered the land back to the heirs of Mrs. Cruthers. The Court said:

"In construing a benevolent statute of the government, made for the benefit of its own citizens, inviting and encouraging them to settle on its distant public lands, the words 'single man,' and 'unmarried man' may, especially if aided by the context and other parts of the statute, be taken in a generic sense. Held, accordingly, that the Fourth Section of the Act of Congress, of September 27th, 1850, granting by way of donation, lands in Oregon Territory, to every white settler or occupant, American half-breed Indians included, embraced within the term *single man* an *unmarried woman.*"

And the attorney, who carried this question to its final success, is now the United States senator elect from Oregon, Hon. J. H. Mitchell, in whom the cause of equal rights to women has an added power on the floor of the United States Senate.

Though the words persons, people, inhabitants, electors, citizens, are all used indiscriminately in the national and state constitutions, there was always a conflict of opinion, prior to the war, as to whether they were synonymous terms, as for instance:

"No *person* shall be a *representative* who shall not have been seven years a *citizen*, and who shall not, when elected, be an *inhabitant* of that state in which he is chosen. No *person* shall be a senator who shall not have been a *citizen* of the United States, and an *inhabitant* of that state in which he is chosen."

But, whatever room there was for a doubt, under the old regime, the adoption of the fourteenth amendment settled that question forever, in its first sentence: "All persons born or naturalized in the United States and subject to the jurisdiction thereof, are citizens of the United States and of the state wherein they reside."

And the second settles the equal status of all persons—all citizens:

"No state shall make or enforce any law which shall abridge the privileges or immunities of citizens; nor shall any state deprive any person of life, liberty or property, without due process of law, nor deny to any person within its jurisdiction the equal protection of the laws."

The only question left to be settled, now, is: Are women persons? And I hardly believe any of our opponents will have the hardihood to say they are not. Being persons, then, women are citizens, and no state has a right to make any new law, or to enforce any old law, that shall abridge their privileges or immunities. Hence, every discrimination against women in the constitutions and laws of the several states, is to-day null and void, precisely as is every one against negroes.

Is the right to vote one of the privileges or immunities of citizens? I think the disfranchised ex-rebels, and the ex-state prisoners will all agree with me, that it is not only one of them, but the one without which all the others are nothing. Seek first the kingdom of the ballot, and all things else shall be given thee, is the political injunction.

Webster, Worcester and Bouvier all define citizen to be a person, in the United States, entitled to vote and hold office.

Prior to the adoption of the thirteenth amendment, by which slavery was forever abolished, and black men transformed from property to persons, the judicial opinions of the country had always been in harmony with these definitions. To be a person was to be a citizen, and to be a citizen was to be a voter.

Associate Justice Washington, in defining the privileges and immunities of the citizen, more than fifty years ago, said: "they included all such privileges as were fundamental in their nature. And among them is the right to exercise the elective franchise, and to hold office."

Even the "Dred Scott" decision, pronounced by the abolitionists and republicans infamous, because it virtually declared "black men had no rights white men were bound to respect," gave this true and logical conclusion, that to be one of the people was to be a citizen and a voter.

Chief Judge Daniels said:

"There is not, it is believed, to be found in the theories of writers on government, or in any actual experiment heretofore tried, an exposition of the term citizen, which has not been considered as conferring the actual possession and enjoyment of the perfect right of acquisition and enjoyment of an entire equality of privileges, civil and political."

Associate Justice Taney said:

"The words 'people of the United States,' and 'citizens,' are synonymous terms, and mean the same thing. They both describe the political body, who, according to our republican institutions, form the sovereignty, and who hold the power and conduct the government, through their representatives. They are what we familiarly call the sovereign people, and every citizen is one of this people, and a constituent member of this sovereignty."

Thus does Judge Taney's decision, which was such a terrible ban to the black man, while he was a slave, now, that he is a person, no longer property, pronounce him a citizen, possessed of an entire equality of privileges, civil and political. And not only the black man, but the black woman, and all women as well.

And it was not until after the abolition of slavery, by which the negroes became free men, hence citizens, that the United States Attorney, General Bates, rendered a contrary opinion. He said:

"The constitution uses the word 'citizen' only to express the political quality, (not equality mark,) of the individual in his relation to the nation; to declare that he is a member of the body politic, and bound to it by the reciprocal obligations of allegiance on the one side, and protection on the other. The phrase, 'a citizen of the United States,' without addition or qualification, means neither more nor less than a member of the nation."

Then, to be a citizen of this republic, is no more than to be a subject of an empire. You and I, and all true and patriotic citizens must repudiate this base conclusion. We all know that American citizenship, without addition or qualification, means the possession of equal rights, civil and political. We all know that the crowning glory of every citizen of the United States is, that he can either give or withhold his vote from every law and every legislator under the government.

Did "I am a Roman citizen," mean nothing more than that I am a "member" of the body politic of the republic of Rome, bound to it by the reciprocal obligations of allegiance on the one side, and protection on the other? Ridiculously absurd question, you say. When you, young man, shall travel abroad, among the monarchies of the old world, and there proudly boast yourself an "American citizen," will you thereby declare yourself neither more nor less than a "member" of the American nation?

And this opinion of Attorney General Bates, that a black citizen was not a voter, made merely to suit the political exigency of the republican party, in that transition hour between emancipation and enfranchisement, was no less infamous, in spirit or purpose, than was the decision of Judge

Taney, that a black man was not one of the people, rendered in the interest and at the behest of the old democratic party, in its darkest hour of subjection to the slave power. Nevertheless, all of the adverse arguments, adverse congressional reports and judicial opinions, thus far, have been based on this purely partisan, time-serving opinion of General Bates, that the normal condition of the citizen of the United States is that of disfranchisement. That only such classes of citizens as have had special legislative guarantee have a legal right to vote.

And if this decision of Attorney General Bates was infamous, as against black men, but yesterday plantation slaves, what shall we pronounce upon Judge Bingham, in the house of Representatives, and Carpenter, in the Senate of the United States, for citing it aganist the women of the entire nation, vast numbers of whom are the peers of those honorable gentlemen, themselves, in morals!! intellect, culture, wealth, family—paying taxes on large estates, and contributing equally with them and their sex, in every direction, to the growth, prosperity and well-being of the republic? And what shall be said of the judicial opinions of Judges Carter, Jameson, McKay and Sharswood, all based upon this aristocratic, monarchial idea, of the right of one class to govern another?

I am proud to mention the names of the two United States Judges who have given opinions honorable to our republican idea, and honorable to themselves—Judge Howe, of Wyoming Territory, and Judge Underwood, of Virginia.

The former gave it as his opinion a year ago, when the Legislature seemed likely to revoke the law enfranchising the women of that territory, that, in case they succeeded, the women would still possess the right to vote under the fourteenth amendment.

Judge Underwood, of Virginia, in noticing the recent decision of Judge Carter, of the Supreme Court of the District of Columbia, denying to women the right to vote, under the fourteenth and fifteenth amendment, says;

"If the people of the United States, by amendment of their constitution, could expunge, without any explanatory or assisting legislation, an adjective of five letters from all state and local constitutions, and thereby raise millions of our most ignorant fellow-citizens to all of the rights and privileges of electors, why should not the same people, by the same amendment, expunge an adjective of four letters from the same state and local constitutions, and thereby raise other millions of more educated and better informed citizens to equal rights and privileges, without explanatory or assisting legislation ?"

If the fourteenth amendment does not secure to all citizens the right to vote, for what purpose was that grand old charter of the fathers lumbered with its unwieldy proportions? The republican party, and Judges Howard and Bingham, who drafted the document, pretended it was to do something for black men; and if that something was not to secure them in their right to vote and hold office, what could it have been? For, by the thirteenth amendment, black men had become people, and hence were entitled to all the privileges and immunities of the government, precisely as were the women of the country, and foreign men not naturalized. According to Associate Justice Washington, they already had the

"Protection of the government, the enjoyment of life and liberty, with the right to acquire and possess property of every kind, and to pursue and obtain happiness and safety, subject to such restraints as the government may justly prescribe for the general welfare of the whole; the right of a citizen of one state to pass through or to reside in any other state for the purpose of trade, agriculture, professional pursuit, or otherwise; to claim the benefit of the writ of habeas corpus, to institute and maintain actions of any kind in the courts of the state; to take, hold, and dispose of property, either real or personal, and an exemption from higher taxes or impositions than are paid by the other citizens of the state."

Thus, you see, those newly freed men were in possession of every possible right, privilege and immunity of the government, except that of suffrage, and hence, needed no constitutional amendment for any other purpose. What right, I ask you, has the Irishman the day after he receives his naturalization papers that he did not possess the day before, save the right to vote and hold office? And the Chinamen, now crowding our Pacific coast, are in precisely the same position. What privilege or immunity has California or Oregon the constitutional right to deny them, save that of the ballot? Clearly, then, if the fourteenth amendment was not to secure to black men their right to vote, it did nothing for them, since they possessed everything else before. But, if it was meant to be a prohibition of the states, to deny or abridge their right to vote—which I fully believe—then it did the same for all persons, white women included, born or naturalized in the United States; for the amendment does not say all male persons of African descent, but all persons are citizens.

The second section is simply a threat to punish the states, by reducing their representation on the floor of Congress, should they disfranchise any of their male citizens, on account of color, and does not allow of the inference that the states may disfranchise from any, or all other causes; nor in any wise weaken or invalidate the universal guarantee of the first section. What rule of law or logic would allow the conclusion, that the prohibition of a crime to one person, on severe pains and penalties, was a sanction of that crime to any and all other persons save that one?

But, however much the doctors of the law may disagree, as to whether people and citizens, in the original constitution, were one and the same, or whether the privileges and immunities in the fourteenth amendment include the right of suffrage, the question of the citizen's right to vote is settled forever by the fifteenth amendment. "The citizen's right to vote shall not be denied by the United States, nor any state thereof; on account of race, color, or previous condition of servitude." How can the state deny or abridge the right of the citizen, if the citizen does not possess it? There is no escape from the conclusion, that to vote is the citizen's right, and the specifications of race, color, or previous condition of servitude can, in no way, impair the force of the emphatic assertion, that the citizen's right to vote shall not be denied or abridged.

The political strategy of the second section of the fourteenth amendment, failing to coerce the rebel states into enfranchising their negroes, and the necessities of the republican party demanding their votes throughout the South, to ensure the re-election of Grant in 1872, that party was compelled to place this positive prohibition of the fifteenth amendment upon the United States and all the states thereof.

If we once establish the false principle, that United States citizenship does not carry with it the right to vote in every state in this Union, there is no end to the petty freaks and cunning devices, that will be resorted to, to exclude one and another class of citizens from the right of suffrage.

It will not always be men combining to disfranchise all women; native born men combining to abridge the rights of all naturalized citizens, as in Rhode Island. It will not always be the rich and educated who may combine to cut off the poor and ignorant; but we may live to see the poor, hard-working, uncultivated day laborers, foreign and native born, learning the power of the ballot and their vast majority of numbers, combine and amend state constitutions so as to disfranchise the Vanderbilts and A. T. Stewarts, the Conklings and Fentons. It is a poor rule that won't work more ways than one. Establish this precedent, admit the right to deny suffrage to the states, and there is no power to foresee the confusion, discord and disruption that may await us. There is, and can be, but one safe principle of government—equal rights to all. And any and every discrimination against any class, whether on account of color, race, nativity, sex, property, culture, can but imbitter and disaffect that class, and thereby endanger the safety of the whole people.

Clearly, then, the national government must not only define the rights of citizens, but it must stretch out its powerful hand and protect them in every state in this Union.

But if you will insist that the fifteenth amendment's emphatic interdiction against robbing United States citizens of their right to vote, "on account of race, color, or previous condition of servitude," is a recognition of the right, either of the United States, or any state, to rob citizens of that right, for any or all other reasons, I will prove to you that the class of citizens for which I now plead, and to which I belong, may be, and are, by all the principles of our government, and many of the laws of the states, included under the term "previous condition of servitude."

First.—The married women and their legal status. What is servitude? "The condition of a slave." What is a slave? "A person who is robbed of the proceeds of his labor; a person who is subject to the will of another."

By the law of Georgia, South Carolina, and all the states of the South, the negro had no right to the custody and control of his person. He belonged to his master. If he was disobedient, the master had the right to use correction. If the negro didn't like the correction, and attempted to run away, the master had a right to use coercion to bring him back.

By the law of every state in this Union to-day, North as well as South, the married woman has no right to the custody and control of her person. The wife belongs to her husband; and if she refuses obedience to his will, he may use moderate correction, and if she doesn't like his moderate correction, and attempts to leave his "bed and board," the husband may use moderate coercion to bring her back. The little word "moderate," you see, is the saving clause for the wife, and would doubtless be overstepped should her offended husband administer his correction with the "cat-o'-nine-tails," or accomplish his coercion with blood-hounds.

Again, the slave had no right to the earnings of his hands, they belonged to his master; no right to the custody of his children, they belonged to his master; no right to sue or be sued, or testify in the courts. If he committed a crime, it was the master who must sue or be sued.

In many of the states there has been special legislation, giving to married women the right to property inherited, or received by bequest, or earned by the pursuit of any avocation outside of the home; also, giving her the right to sue and be sued in matters pertaining to such separate property; but not a single state of this Union has ever secured the wife in the enjoyment of her right to the joint ownership of the joint earnings of the marriage copartnership. And since, in the nature of things, the vast majority of married women never earn a dollar, by work outside of their families, nor inherit a dollar from their fathers, it follows that from the day of their marriage to the day of the death of their husbands, not one of them ever has a dollar, except it shall please her husband to *let* her have it.

In some of the states, also, there have been laws passed giving to the mother a joint right with the father in the guardianship of the children. But twenty years ago, when our woman's rights movement commenced, by the laws of the State of New York, and all the states, the father had the sole custody and control of the children. No matter if he were a brutal, drunken libertine, he had the legal right, without the mother's consent, to apprentice her sons to rumsellers, or her daughters to brothel keepers. He could even will away an unborn child, to some other person than the mother. And in many of the states the law still prevails, and the mothers are still utterly powerless under the common law.

I doubt if there is, to-day, a State in this Union where a married woman can sue or be sued for slander of character, and until quite recently there was not one in which she could sue or be sued for injury of person. However damaging to the wife's reputation any slander may be, she is wholly powerless to institute legal proceedings against her accuser, unless her husband shall join with her; and how often have we heard of the husband conspiring with some outside barbarian to blast the good name of his wife? A married woman cannot testify in courts in cases of joint interest with her husband. A good farmer's wife near Earlville, Ill., who had all the rights she wanted, went to a dentist of the village and had a full set of false teeth, both upper and under. The dentist pronounced them an admirable fit, and the wife declared they gave her fits to wear them; that she could neither chew nor talk with them in her mouth. The dentist sued the husband; his counsel brought the wife as witness; the judge ruled her off the stand, saying "a married woman cannot be a witness in matters of joint interest between herself and her husband." Think of it, ye good wives, the false teeth in your mouths are joint interest with your husbands, about which you are legally incompetent to speak!! If in our frequent and shocking railroad accidents a married woman is injured in her person, in nearly all of the States, it is her husband who must sue the company, and it is to her husband that the damages, if there are any, will be awarded. In Ashfield, Mass., supposed to be the most advanced of any State in the Union in all things, humanitarian as well as intellectual, a married woman was severely injured by a defective sidewalk. Her husband sued the corporation and recovered $13,000 damages. And those $13,000 belong to him *bona fide;* and whenever that unfortunate wife wishes a dollar of it to supply her needs she must ask her husband for it; and if the man be of a narrow, selfish, niggardly nature, she will have to hear him say, every time, "What have you done, my dear, with the twenty-five cents I gave you yesterday?" Isn't such a position, I ask you, humiliating enough to be called "servitude?" That husband, as would any other husband, in nearly every State of this Union, sued and obtained damages for the loss of the services of his wife, precisely as the master, under the old slave regime, would have done, had his slave been thus injured, and precisely as he himself would have done had it been his ox, cow or horse instead of his wife.

There is an old saying that "a rose by any other name would smell as sweet," and I submit if the deprivation by law of the ownership of one's own person, wages, property, children, the denial of the right as an individual, to sue and be sued, and to testify in the courts, is not a condition of servitude most bitter and absolute, though under the sacred name of marriage?

Does any lawyer doubt my statement of the legal status of married women? I will remind him of the fact that the old common law of England prevails in every State in this Union, except where the Legislature has enacted special laws annulling it. And I am ashamed that not one State has yet blotted from its statute books the old common law of marriage, by which Blackstone, summed up in the fewest words possible, is made to say, "husband and wife are one, and that one is the husband."

Thus may all married women, wives and widows, by the laws of the several States, be technically included in the fifteenth amendment's specification of "condition of servitude," present or previous. And not only married women, but I will also prove to you that by all the great fundamental principles of our free government, the entire womanhood of the nation is in a "condition of servitude" as surely as were our revolutionary fathers, when they rebelled against old King George. Women are taxed without representation, governed without their consent, tried, convicted and punished without a jury of their peers. And is all this tyranny any less humiliating and degrading to women under our democratic-republican government to-day than it was to men under their aristocratic, monarchical government one hundred years ago? There is not an utterance of old John Adams, John Hancock or Patrick Henry, but finds a living response in the soul of every intelligent, patriotic woman of the nation. Bring to me a common-sense woman property holder, and I will show you one whose soul is fired with all the indignation of 1776 every time the tax-gatherer presents himself at her door. You will not find one such but feels her condition of servitude as galling as did James Otis when he said:

"The very act of taxing exercised over those who are not represented appears to me to be depriving them of one of their most essential rights, and if continued, seems to be in effect an entire disfranchisement of every civil right. For, what one civil right is worth a rush after a man's property is subject to be taken from him at pleasure without his consent? If a man is not his own assessor in person, or by deputy, his liberty is gone, or he is wholly at the mercy of others."

What was the three-penny tax on tea, or the paltry tax on paper and sugar to which our revolutionary fathers were subjected, when compared with the taxation of the women of this Republic? The orphaned Pixley sisters, six dollars a day, and even the women, who are proclaiming the tyranny of our taxation without representation, from city to city throughout the country, are often compelled to pay a tax for the poor privilege of defending our rights. And again, to show that disfranchisement was precisely the slavery of which the fathers complained, allow me to cite to you old Ben. Franklin, who in those olden times was admitted to be good authority, not merely in domestic economy, but in political as well; he said:

"Every man of the commonalty, except infants, insane persons and criminals, is, of common right and the law of God, a freeman and entitled to the free enjoyment of liberty.

That liberty or freedom consists in having an actual share in the appointment of those who are to frame the laws, and who are to be the guardians of every man's life, property and peace. For the all of one man is as dear to him as the all of another; and the poor man has an equal right, but more need to have representatives in the Legislature than the rich one. That they who have no voice or vote in the electing of representatives, do not enjoy liberty, but are absolutely enslaved to those who have votes and their representatives; for to be enslaved is to have governors whom other men have set over us, and to be subject to laws made by the representatives of others, without having had representatives of our own to give consent in our behalf."

Suppose I read it with the feminine gender:

"That women who have no voice nor vote in the electing of representatives, do not enjoy liberty, but are absolutely enslaved to men who have votes and their representatives; for to be enslaved is to have governors whom men have set over us, and to be subject to the laws made by the representatives of men, without having representatives of our own to give consent in our behalf."

And yet one more authority; that of Thomas Paine, than whom not one of the Revolutionary patriots more ably vindicated the principles upon which our government is founded:

"The right of voting for representatives is the primary right by which other rights are protected. To take away this right is to reduce man to a state of slavery; for slavery consists in being subject to the will of another; and he that has not a vote in the election of representatives is in this case. The proposal, therefore, to disfranchise any class of men is as criminal as the proposal to take away property."

Is anything further needed to prove woman's condition of servitude sufficiently orthodox to entitle her to the guaranties of the fifteenth amendment?

Is there a man who will not agree with me, that to talk of freedom without the ballot, is mockery—is slavery—to the women of this Republic, precisely as New England's orator

Wendell Phillips, at the close of the late war, declared it to be to the newly emancipated black men?

I admit that prior to the rebellion, by common consent, the right to enslave, as well as to disfranchise both native and foreign born citizens, was conceded to the States. But the one grand principle, settled by the war and the reconstruction legislation, is the supremacy of national power to protect the citizens of the United States in their right to freedom and the elective franchise, against any and every interference on the part of the several States. And again and again, have the American people asserted the triumph of this principle, by their overwhelming majorities for Lincoln and Grant.

The one issue of the last two Presidential elections was, whether the fourteenth and fifteenth amendments should be considered the irrevocable will of the people; and the decision was, they shall be—and that it is not only the right, but the duty of the National Government to protect all United States citizens in the full enjoyment and free exercise of all their privileges and immunities against any attempt of any State to deny or abridge.

And in this conclusion Republicans and Democrats alike agree.

Senator Frelinghuysen said:

"The heresy of State rights has been completely buried in these amendments, that as amended, the Constitution confers not only national but State citizenship upon all persons born or naturalized within our limits."

The Call for the national Republican convention said:

"Equal suffrage has been engrafted on the national Constitution; the privileges and immunities of American citizenship have become a part of the organic law."

The national Republican platform said:

"Complete liberty and exact equality in the enjoyment of all civil, political and public rights, should be established and maintained throughout the Union by efficient and appropriate State and federal legislation."

If that means anything, it is that Congress should pass a law to require the States to protect women in their equal political rights, and that the States should enact laws making it the duty of inspectors of elections to receive women's votes on precisely the same conditions they do those of men.

Judge Stanley Mathews—a substantial Ohio democrat—in his preliminary speech at the Cincinnati convention, said most emphatically:

"The constitutional amendments have established the political equality of all citizens before the law."

President Grant, in his message to Congress March 30th, 1870, on the adoption of the fifteenth amendment, said:

"A measure which makes at once four millions of people voters, is indeed a measure of greater importance than any act of the kind from the foundation of the Government to the present time."

How could *four* millions negroes be made voters if *two* millions were not included?

The California State Republican convention said:

"Among the many practical and substantial triumphs of the principles achieved by the Republican party during the past twelve years, it enumerated with pride and pleasure, the prohibiting of any State from abridging the privileges of any citizen of the Republic, the declaring the civil and political equality of every citizen, and the establishing all these principles in the federal constitution by amendments thereto, as the permanent law."

Benjamin F. Butler, in a recent letter to me, said:

"I do not believe anybody in Congress doubts that the Constitution authorizes the right of women to vote, precisely as it authorizes trial by jury and many other like rights guaranteed to citizens."

And again, General Butler said:

"It is not laws we want; there are plenty of laws—good enough, too. Administrative ability to enforce law is the great want of the age, in this country especially. Everybody talks of law, law. If everybody would insist on the enforcement of law, the government would stand on a firmer basis, and questions would settle themselves."

And it is upon this just interpretation of the United States Constitution that our National Woman Suffrage Association which celebrates the twenty-fifth anniversary of the woman's rights movement in New York on the 6th of May next, has based all its arguments and action the past five years.

We no longer petition Legislature or Congress to give us the right to vote. We appeal to the women everywhere to exercise their too long neglected "citizen's right to vote." We appeal to the inspectors of election everywhere to receive the votes of all United States citizens as it is their duty to do. We appeal to United States commissioners and marshals to arrest the inspectors who reject the names and votes of United States citizens, as it is their duty to do, and leave those alone who, like our eighth ward inspectors, perform their duties faithfully and well.

We ask the juries to fail to return verdicts of "guilty" against honest, law-abiding, tax-paying United States citizens for offering their votes at our elections. Or against intelligent, worthy young men, inspectors of elections, for receiving and counting such citizens' votes.

We ask the judges to render true and unprejudiced opinions of the law, and wherever there is room for a doubt to give its benefit on the side of liberty and equal rights to women, remembering that "the true rule of interpretation under our national constitution, especially since its amendments, is that anything for human rights is constitutional, everything against human rights unconstitutional."

And it is on this line that we propose to fight our battle for the ballot—all peaceably, but nevertheless persistently through to complete triumph, when all United States citizens shall be recognized as equals before the law.

SPEECH OF

MATILDA JOSLYN GAGE,

In Canandaigua and 16 other towns of Ontario county, previous to Miss Anthony's Trial, June 17th, 1873.

THE UNITED STATES ON TRIAL;

not

SUSAN B. ANTHONY.

Governments derive their just powers from the consent of the governed. That is the axiom of our republic. From this axiom we understand that powers used by the government without the consent of the governed, are *not just* powers, but that on the contrary, they are *unjust* powers, *usurped* powers, *illegal* powers.

In what way does the consent of the governed come?

By and through the ballot alone. The ballot answers questions. It says yes, or no. It declares what *principles* shall rule; it says what *laws* shall be made, it tells what *taxes* are to be raised; it places men in office or lays their heads low in the dust. It is the *will* of a man embodied in that little piece of paper; it is the consent of the governed.

Are women governed? Most certainly; they pay taxes,—they are held amenable to laws; they are tried for crimes; they are fined, imprisoned, hung. The government wields strong power over them. Have they consented to this power of the government? Have they a recognized right to the ballot? Has their consent been asked through their votes? Have they had a voice in saying what taxes shall be levied on their property,—what penalties they shall pay for crimes? *No.* They are ruled without their consent. The first principles of government are founded on the natural rights of individuals; in order to *secure* the exercise of these natural, individual rights our government professed to be founded. Governments never created a single right; rights did not come new-born into the world with our revolutionary fathers. They were men of middle age when they severed their connexion with Great Britain, but that severance did not endow them with a single new right. It was at that time they first entered into the *exercise* of their natural, individual rights. Neither our Declaration, nor our Constitution created a single right; they merely recognized certain rights as in existence. They recognized those rights as human rights,—as inalienable rights,—as rights existing by virtue of common humanity. Natural rights never change, but the power to perceive these natural rights does change, and various nations have had their own standard.

Three names, said to be the sweetest the world ever knew, are mother, home, and heaven. There is one still sweeter—one for which men have given up mother and home, and for which they have almost sacrificed the hope of heaven; that word is LIBERTY.

When the fires of liberty began to creep through Europe in the middle ages, at a time whon hereditary monarchs and the catholic church ruled the world, men placed its safeguards in municipal corporations. The idea of municipal corporations descended from Rome to the rest of Europe, and "free cities" became the germ of personal freedom. But a new world was needed for the great experiment of individual freedom. Macauley calls government an experimental science and therefore a progressive science; history shows this to be true. Liberty did not spring "full armed" like Minerva from the head of Jove. The liberty possessed by the world has been gradually secured, and it was left for our country first to incorporate in its foundation a recognition of individual rights. A hundred years before the revolutionary war, Massachusetts and Virginia resisted English tyranny. Massachusetts, in 1664, called herself a "perfect republic." She preserved a neutral harbor by force of arms against opposing English factions; she enacted laws against the supremacy of the English parliament, and she established her own mint. This last is noticeable, as in the progress of liberty, rights of property, of which money is the exponent, have always been one of the foremost. Bancroft says Virginia was always a land of liberty; that Virginia placed the defense of liberty not in municipal corporations, *but in persons,* and that the liberty of the individual was ever highly prized. The difference between a monarchy and a republic is the difference between force and consent; it is the difference between being governed and governing yourself; it is the difference between the *men* of Russia and the *men* of the United States; it is the difference between the political rights of one man as the government and the political rights of the people as the government. But the world has never yet seen a true republic, though it has for hundreds of years been taking steps towards one.

The original principles of just governments are five, all of which were acknowledged by the United States at its foundation. These principles are:

First. The natural right of each individual to self-government.

Second. The exact equality of these rights.

Third. That these rights when not delegated by the individual, are retained by the individual.

Fourth. That no person can exercise these rights of others without delegated authority.

Fifth. That the non-use of these rights does not destroy them.

These five underlying principles are the admitted basis of all governmental rights, and the old revolutionists acted upon them. They were men of middle life; they were under an old and established form of government to which they had not delegated authority, and during all these years they had made no use of their natural, equal rights. When they chose to assume the exercise of these rights, they at once took them up.

The women of that day were no less in earnest than were the men. Mercy Otis Warren, sister of that James Otis whose fiery words did so much towards rousing the colonies, was herself no less in earnest, had no less influence than her brother. She was a member of the famous committee of correspondence, and was constantly consulted by Adams, Jefferson, Franklin, Hancock, Washington and all the foremost men of that day. Through her lips was first whispered the word, separation. No less active were the women of New England, and in 1770, five years before the breaking out of the revolutionary war, the women of Boston held a public meeting, and formed themselves into a league to resist taxation. As tea was the article upon which Great Britain was then making her stand, in order to sustain the *principle* of taxation, these women declared they would use no more tea until the tax upon it was repealed. This league was first formed by the married women, but the next day the young women met "in innumerable numbers," and took similar action. They expressly stated, they did not do this so much for themselves, as for the benefit of their posterity. In the country, the women of that hour went abroad over the fields and sowed their tea, as men sow wheat. This action of the women of the revolution was taken three years before the famous Tea Party of Boston harbor, and was the real origin of that "Tea Party." The women of the present day, the "posterity" of these women of the revolution, are now following the example then set, and are protesting against taxation without representation. A few weeks ago I attended a meeting of the tax-paying women of Rochester who met in the Mayor's office in that city, and there, like their revolutionary mothers, formed a league against taxation without representation. Meetings for the discussion of measures are regularly held by them, and they have issued an address, which I will read you.

To the Women of the City of Rochester and the County of Monroe:

After twenty-five years of discussion, appeal and work, the Women of Rochester assembled, are prompted to advise and urge taxpaying women of the City and County, that the time has come to act, as our patriot mothers acted in 1770, *in protest against unjust government,* and the action appropriate and suited to the time, is strong and earnest protest against the violation of the Republican principles, which compels the payment of taxes by women, while they are denied the ballot.

By order of "THE WOMEN TAX PAYERS' ASSOCIATION of the City of Rochester and County of Monroe."

They have also issued this memorial and protest, addressed

To the Board of Supervisors of the County of Monroe, and to the Hon. the Common Council of the City of Rochester:

The payment of taxes is exacted in direct violation of the principles that "Governments derive their just powers from the consent of the governed," and that "there shall be no taxation without representation." Therefore we earnestly protest against the payment of taxes, either Municipal, County, or State, until the ballot secures us in the right of representation, just and equal with other citizens.

By order of "THE WOMEN TAX PAYERS' ASSOCIATION of the City of Rochester and County of Monroe."

Thus women are everywhere going back to fundamental principles, and this action of the women of Rochester is but the commencement of a protest which will soon become a resistance, and which will extend from the St. Lawrence to the Gulf of Mexico, from the Atlantic to the Pacific. The women of the city of Rochester pay taxes on seven millions of property, and yet not one of these tax payers is consulted as to how, or when that tax shall be raised, or for what purpose used. This seven millions is but a small proportion of property on which the women of that city really pay taxes, as it does not include that much larger amount of property of which they have been robbed, and over which they are assumed to have no control. The foundation of a new city hall has recently been laid in that city. Women's property, without their consent, has been used for this purpose. Water is soon to be brought in from Hemlock Lake, and a dozen other projects are on foot, all of which require money, and towards all of which, the money of tax-paying women will be taken without their consent.

To illustrate the extreme injustice with which women are treated in this matter of taxation, to show you how contrary it is to all natural right, let us suppose that all the taxable property in the city of Rochester belonged to women, with the exception of a single small house and lot, which were owned by a man. As the law is now interpreted, the man who owned that house and lot could vote a tax upon the property of all those women at his own will, to build CITY HALLS, COURT HOUSES, JAILS, could call an election and vote an extraordinary tax to bring in water from a dozen different lakes, erect fountains at every corner, fence in twenty parks, vote himself in, Mayor, Alderman, Assessor, Collector with a fat salary from these women's money, attached to each one of these offices, and in the end elect himself the sole policeman of the city, to protect the women from—himself; and this you call just government. It is no more unjust, no more unrepublican, to take the property of fifty, or a hundred, or a thousand women in this way, than it would be to take the property of a single one; the principle is still the same. The women of to-day, protest, as did their fore-mothers, for principle. Women come into the world endowed with the same natural rights as men, and this by virtue of their common humanity, and when prevented or restrained from their exercise, they are enslaved. Old Ben Franklin once said, "those that have no vote or voice in the laws, or the election of those who administer them, do not enjoy liberty, but are *absolutely enslaved* to those who have votes, and their representatives." That sentiment is as true to-day as when uttered. While the women of this nation are restrained from the exercise of their natural rights of self-government, they are held enslaved to those who do administer the laws. Said an old minister of revolutionary fame, "One who is bound to obey the will of another is as really a slave, though he may have a good master, as if he had a bad one." Those of you who remember Adolph in Uncle Tom's Cabin, will recall his apparent freedom. Dressed in style, wearing his master's garments before the first gloss was off, viewing Uncle Tom, superciliously through his eye glass, he was a petted companion of his master and did not feel his bonds. But one day the scene changed. St. Clair died, and poor Adolph, stripped of all his favors, was dragged off to the vile slave pen. Do you see no parallel between Adolph and the women of America? Adolph was restrained by unjust power from exercise of his natural rights, so are the women of this country, as is most fully shown, by this prosecution and trial of Susan B. Anthony.

In this country, two kinds of representation exist, property and personal. Let us look for a moment, at the Constitution of the United States. In three years we celebrate our centennial. From what does it date? Not from the Constitution, as our country existed eleven years without a Constitution,—in fact, thirteen years, before it was ratified by the thirteen colonies. The centennial dates from the declaration of Independence, which was based on underlying principles. But as our government has recognized its own needs, it has thrown new safeguards around liberty. Within a year after the Declaration, it was found necessary to enter into articles of Confederation, and those were soon followed by the Constitution, as it was found property rights were not secure "under the action of thirteen different deliberatives."

England has never possessed personal representation, but only that of property; and in the secret proceedings upon the framing of our Constitution, the question as to property, or personal representation was strongly agitated. Some of the delegates favored the fuller representation of property than of persons. Others, who advocated the equality of suffrage, took the matter up on the original principles of government, recognizing the fact that it was not strength, or wisdom, or property, that conferred rights, but that "in a state of nature, before any government is formed, all persons are equally free and independent, no one having any right or authority to exercise power over another," and this, without any regard to difference in personal strength, understanding or wealth. It was also argued, and upon this acknowledgment the Constitution was based, "that when individuals enter into government they have *each* a right to an equal voice in its first formation, and afterwards have *each* a right to an equal vote in every matter which relates to their government. That if it could be done conveniently, they have a right to exercise it in person. When it cannot be done in person, but for convenience, representatives are appointed to act for them, every person has a right to an equal vote in choosing that representative, who is intrusted to do for the whole, that which, the whole, if they could assemble, might do in person, and in the transaction of which they would have an equal voice."

This was the basis upon which the Constitution was established, and these, the principles which led to its adoption; principles which include the full recognition of each person as possessed of the inalienable right of self-government.

The argument for equality was continued in the following strain, as reported by one of the delegates, to the Legislature of Maryland: "That if we were to admit, because a man was more wise, more strong, more wealthy, he should be entitled to more votes than another, it would be inconsistent with the freedom of that other, and would reduce him to slavery. The following illustration was used: "Suppose, for instance, *ten individuals* in a state of nature, about to enter into government, nine of whom were equally wise, equally strong, equally wealthy, the tenth is ten times as wise, ten times as strong, or ten times as rich; if, for this reason, he is to have ten votes for each vote of the others, the nine might as well have no vote at all, and though the whole nine might assent to the measure, yet the vote of the tenth would countervail, and set aside all their votes. If this tenth approved of what they wished to adopt, it would be well; but if he disapproved, he could prevent it, and in the same manner he could carry into execution any measure he wished, contrary to the opinion of all the others, he having ten votes, and the others altogether but nine. It is evident that on these principles, the nine would have no will or discretion of their own, but must be totally dependent on the will and discretion of the tenth; to him they would be as absolutely slaves as any negro is to his master. If he did not attempt to carry into execution any measures injurious to the other nine, it could only be said that they had a good master; they would not be the less slaves, because they would be totally dependent upon the will of another and not on their own will. They might not feel their chains, but they would notwithstanding wear them; and whenever their master pleased, he might draw them so tight as to gall them to the bone." Again it was urged that though every individual should have a voice in the government, yet even then, superior wealth, strength, or understanding, would give great and undue advantage to those who possessed them. But the point especially pressed in these debates was that each individual before entering into government, was equally free and independent: and therefore the conclusion was drawn that each person had equal right both at the time of framing a government, and also after a government or constitution was framed.

To those who with old English ideas, constantly pressed property representation, it was replied that "taxation and representation ought to go together in so far that a person not represented ought not to be taxed."

This Constitutional Convention was in session a number of months; its delegates were partially elected by women's votes, as at that date women were exercising their right of self-government through voting, certainly in the States of Massachusetts and New Jersey, if not in Georgia and Delaware. These women sent their delegates or representatives to assist in framing a Constitution.

Let us look at the Preamble of that instrument. It reads thus:

"We, the PEOPLE of the United States, in order to form a more perfect union, establish *justice,* insure domestic tranquility, provide for the *common* welfare, and secure the blessings of liberty to ourselves and our posterity, do ordain and establish this Constitution for the United States of America."

Here we have a statement as to *who* established the Constitution. It was not the thirteen States as States, not the government in its sovereign capacity, but the people: not the white people alone, not the native born alone, not the male people alone, but the people in a collective sense. Justice was not established by this Constitution if one half the people were left out from its provisions, neither was the *common* welfare considered unless all people in common, equally shared the benefits of the Constitution. And moreover, the posterity of the people of that time are female as well as male. Therefore not only by our knowledge of the course of argument taken by the framers of the Constitution, not only by our knowledge that women as well as men helped elect delegates to that convention,—not only from the original principles proclaimed in the Declaration, but also by and through this Preamble to the Constitution do we find woman equally with man, recognized as part of the governing power.

Although women do not rest their claim to self-government upon any human instrument, it is well to show that even in the Declaration, and the original Constitution, the "Constitution as it was," the rights of *all* people were most emphatically and truly recognized.

Judge Story in his commentaries upon the Constitution, says, "The importance of examining *the Preamble* for the purpose of expounding the language of a Statute has always been felt and universally conceded in all judicial proceedings."

Com. on Const., 1, 443-4.

Chief Justice Jay regarded the Preamble of the Constitution of the United States as an authoritative guide to a correct interpretation of that instrument.

2 *Dallas*, 414.

Coke says, "The Preamble of a Statute is a good means to find out the meaning of the Statute, and as it were, a *key* to the understanding thereof."

Blackstone lays it down as a fundamental principle, that we "must argue from generals down to particulars." Here is good legal authority. I have cited men whose opinions are accepted. We have thus argued down from the *generals* of the Declaration and Constitution to the particulars which appertain to each individual alike, and what is the result? Freedom for all; equal rights. We have read the Preamble of the Constitution, and quoted authorities to show in what light it must be read in reference to its following provisions. By its Preamble, the Constitution is shown to make no distinction in favor of sex. From secret debates of the convention which framed it, we find the motives and the arguments of its framers.

The great foundation and key stone alike of our Republican ideas, *of our Constitution*, is *individual, personal representation,* and it is the greatest blessing to the country at large that the question of representation has come up in the person of Miss Anthony. Men are *compelled* to think upon underlying principles. They are compelled to ask themselves where they get either natural or constitutional right to govern women.

From the earliest ages men have queried among themselves as to where lay the governing power. In the time of Abraham, and even now in some parts of the world the Patriarch of the tribe is looked upon as its supreme ruler. Members of Scottish clans to-day, look with more reverence upon their chief, than upon the Queen: they obey his behests sooner than parliamentary laws. Other men have believed the governing power lay in the hands of a select few, an aristocracy, and that these few men could by right make laws to govern the rest. Others again have believed this power vested in a single man called King, or Czar, or Pope, but it was left to our country, and our age, to promulgate the idea that the governing power lay in the *people themselves.* It took men a great many thousand years to discover this pregnant fact, and although our government laid down at the very first, certain underlying truths, it has taken a very long time even for this country to see, and practice these principles; but as men have opened their eyes to liberty there have been constant advances towards securing its full blessings to each and every individual, and in this progress we had first, the Declaration; second, the Articles of Confederation; third, the Constitution; then the ten Conciliatory Amendments, quickly followed by an eleventh and twelfth, each one of these designed to more fully secure liberty to the people, and making fifteen successive steps in the short period of twenty-eight years.

At the time of framing this government women existed as well as men, women are part of the people; the people created the government. Now, when speaking to you to-night, I am speaking to the people of this part of Ontario County, I am not speaking to men alone, I am not speaking to women alone, but to you all as people. When people frame a government the rights not delegated by them to the government, are retained by them, as is declared by the tenth amendment. Now where do men get their constitutional right to govern women? Women have either delegated their right of self-government to certain delegates, by them to be elected according to all the forms of this government, or they have not so delegated their rights of self-government, but have retained them. In either case, according to the genius of our government, what is there to prevent them from exercising these rights any moment they choose, unless it is force? What prevents them unless it is unjust illegal power? The ninth amendment declares that the enumeration of certain rights, shall not be construed to deny, or disparage others retained by the people. Remember what are the foundation principles of just government, principles fully acted upon by the old revolutionists; remember that no government of whatever kind or character can possibly *create* the right of self-government, but only *recognize* rights as existent; remember the non-use of a right does not destroy that right.

I have a natural right to as much fresh air as I can breathe; if you shut me in a close room with door and windows barred, that does not invalidate my right to breathe pure, fresh air.

I have a natural right to obey the dictates of my own conscience, and to worship God as I choose. If you are physically stronger than I am, or if you are legally stronger than I am and use your strength to prevent the exercise of these natural rights, you by no means destroy them. Though I do not use these rights, I still possess them. The framers of this government, the men and the women who voted at that early day had never until then, exercised their natural rights of self-government; when they chose, they took them up.

But people tell us it was not the intention to include women. What then was the intention? Did the framers of the Declaration intend to leave women under the government of Great Britain? Did they intend to set themselves and their male compeers free, and leave women behind, under a monarchy? Were not women intended to be included in the benefits of the constitution?

Oh, but says some one, they were intended to be generally included, but the amendments had nothing to do with them.

Let us look at this. Is it possible to amend a Constitution not in accordance with its underlying principles? It can be repealed, abolished, destroyed, but not *amended; except in accordance with its original character*. The Supreme Court of the United States has declared that the powers of the Constitution are granted by the people, and are to be exercised strictly *on them*, and *for their benefit*.

Story asks, "Who are the parties to this great contract?" and answers the question by saying, "The people of the United States are the parties to the Constitution."

Com. on Con.

Com. on Con. Legal Rules, 283, says: "This first paragraph of the Constitution, declaring its ends, is the most vital part of the instrument, revealing its spirit and intent, *and the understanding of its framers.*"

Here we have the recognized legal rule that the understanding or INTENTION of the framers of an instrument is to be found in its first paragraph, and the first paragraph of the Constitution declares it was framed BY THE PEOPLE, and for the purpose of securing the blessings of liberty to themselves and their posterity. The native-born American women of to-day, are the posterity of the framers of the Constitution, which was thus designed for their benefit. The intention to include women is here positive; women are part of the people now, and ever have been. "Rules of legal interpretation are general in their character," and so general has the interpretation of the Constitution been, that not only did the people who framed the Constitution, and their posterity, come in for its blessings, but the people also of every nation and tongue, from continent or isles of the sea, who come to us, are included in its benefits. Who can say our forefathers *intended* to include Chinamen, or Sandwich Islanders, or the Norwegian, Russian, or Italian in its benefits? Yet they do all share in it as soon as they become citizens. How absurd we should think the assertion that it was not the Lord's intention to hold the people of the United States under the law of the Ten Commandments, as they were given to the Jews alone, some four thousand years before the United States existed as a nation. Massachusetts never abolished slavery by legislative act; never intentionally abolished it. In 1780 that State adopted a new Constitution with a Bill of Rights, declaring "All men born free and equal." Upon this, some slaves demanded their freedom, and their masters granted it. The slavery of men and *women*, both, was thus destroyed in Massachusetts without intention on the part of the framers of the Constitution, and this, because it is a legal rule to argue down from generals to particulars, and that the "words of a statute ought not to be interpreted to destroy natural justice;" but as Coke says, "Whenever the question of liberty runs doubtful, *the decision must be given in favor of liberty.*"

Digest C. L.

When a Charter declares "all men born free and equal," it means, intends, and includes all women, too; it means all mankind, and this is the *legal interpretation* of the language.

To go back to the Constitution of the United States, let us examine if women were not intended. The first amendment reads, "Congress shall make no law respecting an establishment of religion, or prohibiting the free exercise thereof, or abridging the freedom of speech, or of the press; or the right of the people peaceably to assemble and to petition the government for a redress of grievances."

No mention is there made of women, but who will deny it was not intended for them to enjoy the right of worshipping as they choose? Were they not to be protected in freedom of speech, and in the right of assembling to petition the government for a redress of grievances? Not a man before me will deny that women were included equally with men in the intention of the framers.

The Sixth Amendment reads, "In all criminal prosecutions, the accused shall enjoy the right to a speedy and public trial, by an impartial jury of the State and District wherein the crime shall have been committed, which District shall have been previously ascertained by law; and to be informed of the nature and cause of the accusation; to be confronted with the witnesses against *him*; to have compulsory processes for obtaining witnesses in *his* favor; and to have the existence of counsel in *his* defense."

The words "him" and "his," are three times mentioned in this amendment, yet no one can be found wild enough to say women were not intended to be included in its benefits. Miss Anthony, herself, has already come under its provisions, and were she denied a speedy and open trial, she could appeal to the protection of this very amendment, which not only does not say women, or her, but does alone say *him* and *his*, and this, notwithstanding the other legal adage, that laws stand as they are written. This whole question of constitutional rights, turns on whether the United States is a nation. If the United States is a nation, it has *national* powers. What is the admitted basis of our nation? We reply, equality of political rights. And what, again, is the basis of political rights? Citizenship. Nothing more, nothing less. National sovereignty is only founded upon the political sovereignty of the individual, and national rights are merely individual rights in a collective form. The acknowledged basis of rights in each and every one of the thirty-seven States, is citizenship,—not State citizenship alone, as that alone cannot exist, but first, national citizenship. *National* rights are the fundamental basis of *State* rights. If this is not true, we are then no nation, but merely a confederacy, held together by our own separate wills, and the South was right in its war of secession. Every sovereign right of the United States exists solely from its existence as a nation.

As the nation has grown to know the needs of liberty, it has from time to time thrown new safeguards around it, as I have shown in its fifteen progressive steps since 1776. For sixty years there was no change. Slavery had cast its blight upon our country, and the struggle was for State supremacy. Men forgot the rights, and need of freedom; but in 1861, the climax was reached, and then came the bitter struggle between state and national power. Although our underlying principles were all right, freedom required new guards, and the right of all men to liberty, was put in a new form. An especial statute or amendment was added to our National Constitution, declaring that involuntary servitude, unless for crime, could not exist in this republic. This statute created no new rights; it merely affirmed and elucidated rights as old as creation, and which, in a general way, had been recognized at the very first foundation of our government—even as far back as the old Articles of Association, before the Declaration of Independence. This amendment was the sixteenth step in *securing* the rights of the people, but it was not enough. Our country differs from every other country, in that we have *two kinds* of citizenship. First, we have national citizenship, based upon equal political rights. A person born a citizen of the United States, is, by the very circumstances of birth, endowed with certain political rights. In this respect, the circumstances of birth are very different from those of a person born in Great Britain. A person born in Great Britain is not endowed with political rights, simply because born in that country. Political rights in Great Britain are not based upon personal rights; they are based upon property rights. In England, persons are not represented; only property is represented. That is the very great political difference between England and the United States. In the United States, representation is based upon individual, personal rights—therefore, every person born in the United States—*every person,*—not every white person, nor every male person, but every person is born with *political* rights. The naturalization of foreigners also secures to them the exercise of political rights, because it secures to them citizenship, and they obtain naturalization through *national* law. The war brought about a distinct and new recognition of the rights of national citizenship. States had assumed to be superior to the nation in this very underlying national basis of voting rights, but when certain States boldly attempted to thwart national power, and vote themselves out of the Union,—when by this attempt they virtually said, there is no nation, a new protection was thrown around individual, personal, political rights, by a seventeenth step, known to the world by the Fourteenth Amendment, which defined, (not created) citizenship. "All persons born or naturalized in the United States, and subject to the jurisdiction thereof, are citizens of the United States and of the State wherein they reside," thus recognizing United States citizenship as the first and superior citizenship.

Miss Anthony was not only *born* in the United States, but the United States also has jurisdiction over her, as is shown by this suit, under which she was arrested in Rochester, and held there to examination in the same little room in which fugitive slaves were once examined. From Rochester she was taken to Albany, from Albany back to Rochester, and now from Rochester to Canandaigua, where she is soon to be tried. She has thus been fully acknowledged by the United States as one of its citizens, and also as a citizen of the State in which she resides.

In order to become a citizen of a State, and enjoy the privileges and immunities of States, a citizen of the United States must reside in a State. Citizenship of the United States secures nothing over the citizenship of other countries, unless it secures the right of self-government. State laws may hereafter regulate suffrage, but the difference between regulating and prohibiting, is as great as the difference between state and national citizenship. The question of the war was the question of State rights; it was the negro, *vs.* State rights, or the power of States over the ballot. The question to-day is, woman, *vs.* United States rights, or the power of the United over the ballot. The moral battle now waging will settle the question of the power of the United States over the rights of citizens. By the civil war, the United States was proven to be stronger than the States. It was proven we were a nation in so far that States were but parts of the whole. The woman question, of which in this pending trial, Miss Anthony stands as the exponent, is to settle the question of United States power over the individual political rights of the people; it is a question of a monarchy or a republic. The United States may usurp power, as did the States, but it has no rights in a sovereign capacity, not given it by the Constitution, or in other words, BY THE PEOPLE. By the Preamble we have discovered *who* are its people, and for *what purpose* its Constitution was instituted. Each and every amendment—the first ten, the eleventh, twelfth, thirteenth, fourteenth, and fifteenth, are only parts of the grand whole, and must, each and every one, be examined in the light of the Preamble.

Each added amendment makes this change in the status of the People, in that it gives new guaranties of freedom, and removes all pretense of right from any existing usurped power. People are slow to comprehend the change which has been effected by the decision as to State rights. One, claims that only the negro, or persons of African descent, were affected by it. Others claim, and among them, some prominent Republicans, that every civil right is by these amendments, thrown under national control. Recently, two or three suits have come before the United States on this apprehension. One of these, known as the Slaughter House Case, came up from New Orleans in the suit of certain persons against the State of Louisiana. A permit had been given certain parties to erect sole buildings for slaughter, and in other ways control that entire business in the city of New Orleans for a certain number of years. A suit upon it was appealed to the Supreme Court of the United States, on the ground of the change in the power of States, by, and through the last three amendments, and on the supposition that all the civil power of the States had thus been destroyed.

The Court decided it had no jurisdiction, though in its decision it proclaimed the far-reaching character of these amendments. In reference to the Thirteenth Amendment, the Court used this language:

" We do not say that no one else but the negro can share in this protection. Both the language *and spirit* of these articles are to have their full and just weight in any question of construction. Undoubtedly while negro slavery alone was in the minds of the Congress which proposed the thirteenth article, it forbids any kind of slavery, now, or hereafter. If Mexican peonage, or the Chinese cooley labor system shall develop slavery of the Mexican or Chinese race within our territory, this amendment may be safely trusted to make it void."

This is the language used by the Supreme Court of the United States in reference to this thirteenth amendment; prohibiting any, *all*, and every kind of slavery, not only now, but in the hereafter, and this, although the decision, also acknowledges the fact that only African slavery *was intended* to be covered by this amendment.

The Court further said, "And so if *other* rights are assailed by the States, *which properly and necessarily fall within the protection of these articles*, that protection will apply, though the party interested may not be of African descent."

What "other rights fall within the protection of these articles?" What "other rights" do these amendments cover? The fourteenth article, after declaring who are citizens of the United States, and of States, still further says, "No State shall make or enforce any law which shall abridge the privileges or immunities of citizens of the United States, nor shall any State deprive any person of life, liberty or property, without due process of law, nor deny to any person within its jurisdiction, the equal protection of the laws." This comprises the first section of that amendment. The jurisdiction and protection of the general government applies to United States citizens. By its prosecution of Miss Anthony, the general government acknowledges her as a citizen of the United States, and what is much more, it acknowledges its own jurisdiction over the ballot—over the chief—chief, did I say,—over the *only* political right of its citizens. This prosecution is an admission of United States jurisdiction, instead of State jurisdiction. This whole amendment, with the exception of the first clause of the first section, which simply declares who are citizens of the United States and States, is directed against the interference of *States* in the rights of citizens. But in Miss Anthony's case, the State of New York has not interfered with her right to vote. She voted under local laws, and the State said not a word,—has taken no action in the case, consequently the United States has had no occasion to interfere on that ground. The question of *State* rights was not as great a question as this: What are United States rights? Can the United States, in its sovereign capacity, overthrow the rights of its own citizens? No, it cannot; for the Fifteenth

Amendment to the Constitution specifically declares "The right of citizens of the United States *to vote,* shall not be denied or abridged by the United States, or by any State, on account of race, color, or previous condition of servitude."

This fifteenth Amendment has been seriously misapprehended by many people, who have understood it to mean that *women* could be excluded from voting, simply because they are women. I have shown you that Statutes and Constitutions are always general in their character; that from generals we must argue down to particulars, and that if there is any doubt as to the interpretation of a statute, it must be defined in the interests of liberty But as to the interpretation of this statute there can be no doubt. Had it read, "The right of citizens of the United States to take out passports, shall not be denied or abridged by the United States, on account of race, color, or previous condition of servitude," no person would interpret it to mean that such right to take out passport could be denied on account of *female* sex, or on account of *male* sex. We will read it now, first in the light of the Declaration; second, in that of the Preamble to the Constitution, and the Constitution itself, and its various amendments, to which I have referred: the first, sixth, ninth and tenth, which would have been interpreted male, had the Constitution meant men alone, but which have always been defined to cover, and include woman—to cover and include the rights of the *whole* people to freedom of conscience, to freedom of speech, to the right of a speedy and public trial, &c., &c., and this, although in the Sixth Amendment, the terms *him* and *his* are alone used. The Courts long ago decided that Statutes were of general bearing, as is fully true of the Declaration and Constitution, which are supreme statutes. The Fifteenth Amendment does not specifically exclude right of male citizens to vote, because they are *male* citizens, therefore, male citizens are of necessity included in the right of voting. It does not specifically exclude female citizens from the right of voting, because they are female citizens, therefore, female citizens are of necessity included in the right of voting—a right which the United States cannot abridge. No male citizen can claim that he, as a male citizen, is included, save by implication, and save on the general grounds that he is not specifically excluded, he is necessarily included.

Can the United States, at pleasure, take from its own citizens the right of voting, or abridge that right? Has it the right to take from citizens of States the right of voting? Are citizens of States simply protected against States, and can the United States now, at will, step in and deny or abridge the right of voting to all its male citizens simply because they are male? If it has that power over its female citizens, it has the same power over its male citizens. You cannot fail to see that the question brought up by Miss Anthony's prosecution and trial *by the United States* for the act of voting, has developed the most important question of United States rights; a larger, most pregnant, more momentous question by far, than that of *State* rights. The liberties of the people are much more closely involved when the United States is the aggressor, than when the States are aggressors.

"The Act to Enforce the right of citizens to vote," declares that CITIZENS shall be entitled and allowed to vote at all elections by the people, in any state, territory, district, county, city, parish, township, school district, municipality, or other territorial division, &c.

This Act was passed *after* the ratification of the Fifteenth Amendment, and is designed to be in accordance with the Constitution. It does not say *black* citizens shall be entitled and allowed to vote; it does not say *male* citizens shall be entitled and allowed to vote—it merely says CITIZENS. It covers the right of women citizens to vote, and yet United States officials claim to find in this very act, their authority for prosecuting Miss Anthony and those fourteen other women citizens of Rochester for the alleged *crime* of voting. When Miss Anthony voted, what did she do? She merely exercised her citizen's right of suffrage—a right to which she, and all women citizens are entitled by virtue of their citizenship in the nation—a right to which they are entitled because individual political rights are the basis of the government. The United States has no other foundation. If that right is trampled upon, we have no nation. We may hang together in a sort of anarchical way for a time, but our dissolution draws near. Can the United States destroy rights on account of sex? In the original Constitution, before even the first ten amendments were added, States were forbidden to pass bills of attainder. By the fourteenth amendment, the right of voting was forbidden to be abridged, *unless for crime.* Is it a crime to be a woman? "In the beginning God created man, male and female, created he them." A bill of attainder inflicts punishment, creates liabilities or *disabitities,* on account of parentage, *birth*, or descent. Do United States officials presume to create a disability, or inflict a punishment, on account of *birth* as a woman, and this in direct defiance of the Constitution? When the Constitution of the United States presents no barrier, no lesser power has such authority. "The Constitution of the United States, *and the laws made in pursuance thereof,* shall be the supreme law of the land."

Says article sixth: "Any law of Congress not made in pursuance of, or in unison with the Constitution, is an illegal and void law." Coke declared an Act of Parliament against Magna Charta was null and void.

But United States officials declare it a crime for a United States citizen to vote. If it is a crime for a native-born citizen, it ought to be a still greater crime for a foreign-born citizen But the fact that citizenship carries with it the right of voting, is shown in the act of naturalization. A foreigner, after a certain length of residence in this country, proceeds to take out papers of citizenship. To become a citizen, is all that he needs to make of him a voter. At one and the same time he picks up a ballot, and his naturalization papers. Nothing more than his becoming a citizen is needed for him to vote—nothing less will answer. Susan B. Anthony is a native-born citizen. She had to take out no papers to make her a citizen—she was born in the United States—she is educated, intelligent, and FREE BORN. Native-born citizenship is generally conceded to be of more value than that which is bought. Do you not remember that when Paul was brought up, preparatory to being scourged, he demanded by what right they scourged him, a Roman citizen. The chief captain said, "I bought this freedom with a great price." Paul replied, "I am free born"; then great fear fell upon the chief captain, and he ordered the bonds removed from Paul. Native-born Roman citizenship was worth as much as that two thousand years ago. To-day, the foreign-born American citizen, who has bought his freedom with a great price, who has left his home and country, and crossed the sea to a strange land, in order that he may find freedom, is held to be superior to "free born" American women citizens.

But Miss Anthony is not battling for herself alone, nor for the woman alone; she stands to-day, the embodiment of Republican principles. The question of to-day, is not has woman a right to vote, but has *any* American citizen, white or black, native-born, or naturalized, a right to vote. The prosecution of Miss Anthony by the United States, for the alleged crime of having cast a vote at the last election, is a positive declaration of the government of the United States that it is a crime to vote. Let that decision be affirmed, and we have no republic; the ballot, the governing power in the hands of every person, is the only true republic. Each person to help make the laws which govern him or her, is the only true democracy. Individual responsiblity, personal representation, exact political equality, are the only stable foundations of a republic, and when the United States makes voting a crime on the part of any free-born, law-abiding citizen, it strikes a blow at its own stability; it is undermining the very foundatious of the republic—it is attempting to overthrow its own Constitution.

Miss Anthony is to-day the representative of liberty; she is to-day battling for the rights of every man, woman and child in the country; she is not only upholding the right of every native-born citizen, but of every naturalized citizen; to-day is at stake in her person, the new-born hopes of foreign lands, the quickened instincts of liberty, so well nigh universal. All these are on trial with her; the destinies of America, the civilization of the world, are in the balance with her as she stands on her defence. If the women of this country are restricted in their right of self-government, what better is it for them to have been born in the United States, than to have been born in Russia, or France, or England, or many another monarchical country? No better; nor as well, as in all these countries, women vote upon certain questions. In Russia, about one-half of the property of the country is in the hands of women, and they vote upon its disposition and control. In France and Sweden, women vote at municipal elections, and in England, every woman householder or rate-payer, votes for city officers, for poor wardens and school commissioners, thus expressing her views as to the education of her children, which is a power not possessed by a single woman of this State of New York, whose boast has been that it leads the legislation of the world in regard to women. Property-holding women in England, vote equally with property-holding men, for every office except Parliamentary, and even that is near at hand, a petition for it of 180,000 names going up last year. England, though a monarchy, is consistent with herself. As the foundation of English representation is property, not persons, property is allowed its representation, whether it is held by man or by woman.

"Are ye not of more value than many sparrows?" said one of old. Is it less pertinent for us to ask if personal representation is not more sacred than property representation? "Where governments lead, there are no revolutions," said the eloquent Castelar. But revolution is imminent in a government like ours, instituted by the people, for the people, in its charters recognizing the most sacred rights of the people, but which, in a sovereign capacity, through its officials, tramples upon the most sacredly secured and guaranteed rights of the people.

The question brought up by this trial is not a woman's rights question, but a citizen's rights question. It is not denied that women are citizens,—it is not denied that Susan B. Anthony was born in the United States, and is therefore a citizen of the United States, and of the State wherein she resides, which is this State of New York. It cannot be denied that she is a person,—one of the people,—there is not a word in the Constitution of the United States which militates against the recognition of woman as a person, as one of the people, as a citizen. The whole question, then, to-day, turns on the power of the United States over the political rights of citizens —the whole question then, to-day, turns on the supreme authority of the National Constitution.

The Constitution recognizes native-born women as citizens, both of the United States, and of the States in which they reside, and the Enforcement Act of 1870, in unison with our national fundamental principles, is entitled "An Act *to enforce the right of citizens of the United States to vote* in the several States of the Union." Out of those three words, "for other purposes," or any provisions of this act included in them, cannot be found authority for restraining any citizen not "guilty of participating in the rebellion, or other crime," from voting, and we brand this prosecution of Miss Anthony by United States officials, under claim of provisions in this act, as *an illegal prosecution—an infamous prosecution*, in direct defiance of national law—dangerous in its principles, tending to subvert a republican form of government, and a direct step, whether so designed or not, to the establishment of a monarchy in this country. Where the right of one individual is attacked, the rights of all are menaced. A blow against one citizen, is a blow against every citizen.

The government has shown itself very weak in prosecuting Miss Anthony. No astute lawyer could be found on a side so pregnant of flaws as this one, were not the plaintiff in the case, the sovereign United States. The very fact of the prosecution is at one and the same time weakness on the part of the government, and an act of unauthorized authority. It is weakness, because by it, the United States comes onto the ground of the defendant, and, at once admits voting is an United States right, because United States rights *are citizens' rights*. By this prosecution, the United States clearly admits that protection of the ballot is an United States duty, instead of a State duty. It is an United States duty instead of a State duty, because voting is an United States right instead of a State right. This prosecution is an open admission by the United States, that voting is a *Constitutional right.*

But the prosecution is also an admission of unauthorized authority in that by it, the United States *discriminates between citizens.* If there is one point of our government more strongly fortified than another, it is that the government is of the PEOPLE. The Preamble of the Constitution, heretofore quoted, *means all the people,* if language has a meaning. *All* the people are citizens, if the fourteenth amendment has any signification at all.

If any minds are so obtuse as not to see that the ballot is an United States right,—if any person before me still claims suffrage as a state right alone, such person certainly cannot fail to see that under his views the United States has been guilty of a high-handed outrage upon Miss Anthony and the fourteen other women whom this great government,—this *big United States* has prosecuted. Under this view of the right of suffrage such person cannot fail to see there has been unauthorized interference by the United States, with the duties and rights of the State of New York. And while Uncle Sam was thus busy last winter over the prosecution of women citizens of the State of New York, the State itself submitted in its Legislature, a resolution looking towards the recognition by the State of the right of tax-paying women to the ballot. Thus at one and the same time was seen the anomaly of a prosecution by the United States of women of the State of New York for an act that New York herself was resolving it right to perform, and which if the ballot is not a constitutional right, the United States has no power over at all.

Look at this prosecution as you will, it presents a fine dilemma to solve; it presents to the country, as never before, the most important and vital question of United States rights; it presents the most important and vital question of unconstitutional power which has grown to such dimensions in the hands of United States officials; and it must bring to people's cognizance the very slight thread by which hangs the security of any citizen's right to the ballot.

Governments try themselves. No government has been stable in the past; all have fallen because all have been one-sided; all have permitted the degradation of woman. Babylon fell; her religion defiled woman; the hand-writing appeared upon the wall, and in a single night she was overthrown. Neither was Rome immortal; her laws were class laws; the rights of humanity were not respected; she underwent many changes, and that vast empire which once ruled the world lives now only in name. Egypt held the wisdom of the world, and as to a certain extent she recognized the equality of woman, her empire endured for ages; at last, she too fell, for her civilization was still an unequal one.

Special laws, or laws specially defined for one particular body of people, on account of race, color, sex, or occupation, is class legislation, and bears the seeds of death within itself. It was the boast of our forefathers, that the rights for which they contended were the rights of human nature. Shall the women of this country forever have cause to say that the declaration and the constitution are specially defined,—are organs of special law?

Where the legislative and executive function of the law are in the hands of a single class, special law, or special renderings of law are the unvarying results. If the constitution of the United States is defined and ruled by United States officials to discriminate between classes of citizens, then the constitution is by them made to be nothing less than an organ of special law, and is held not to sustain the rights of the people. While the class which has usurped the legislative, the executive and the judicial functions of the government, defines political rights to belong to male citizens alone, the women of the United States are under special law; and while thus debarred from exercising their natural right of self-government, they are subjects, not citizens. It matters not if women never voted since the framing of the government, until now, this right has merely been retained by them; it has been held in abeyance, to be exercised by them whenever they chose. The principles advocated by the women to-day are the principles which brought on the revolutionary war, and Miss Anthony and other women associated with her are exponents of the very principles which caused the colonies to rebel against the mother country.

The eyes of all nations are upon us; their hopes of liberty are directed towards us; the United States is now on trial by the light of its own underlying principle. Its assertion of human right to self-government lies a hundred years back of it. The chartered confirmation and renewal of this assertion has come up to our very day, and though all the world looked on and wondered to see us crush the rebellion of '61, it is at this hour,—at this soon coming trial of Miss Anthony at Canandaigua, before the Supreme Court of the Northern District of New York,—it is at this trial that republican institutions will have their grand test, and as the decision is rendered for, or against the political rights of citizenship, so will the people of the United States find themselves free or slaves, and so will the United States have tried itself, and paved its way for a speedy fall, or for a long and glorious continuance.

Miss Anthony is to-day the representative of liberty. In all ages of the world, and during all times, there have been epochs in which some one person took upon their own shoulders the hopes and the sorrows of the world, and in their own person, through many struggles bore them onward. Suddenly or gradually, as the case might be, men found the rugged path made smooth and the way opened for the world's rapid advance. Such an epoch exists now, and such a person is Susan B. Anthony.

To you, men of Ontario county, has come an important hour. The fates have brought about that you, of all the men in this great land, have the responsibility of this trial. To you, freedom has comc looking for fuller acknowledgement, for a wider area in which to work and grow. Your decision will not be for Susan B. Anthony alone; it will be for yourselves and for your children's children to the latest generations. You are not asked to decide a question under favor, but according to the foundation principles of this republic. You will be called upon to decide a question according to our great charters of liberty—the Declaration of Independence and the Constitution of the United States. You are to decide, not only on a question of natural right, but of absolute law, of the supreme law of the land. You are not to decide according to prejudice, but according to the constitution. If your decision is favorable to the defendant, you will sustain the constitution; if adverse, if you are blinded by prejudice; you will not decide against women alone, but against theUnited States as well. No more momentous hour has arisen in the interest of freedom, for the underlying principles of the republic, its warp and woof alike, is the exact and permanent political equality of every citizen of the nation, whether that citizen is native born or naturalized, white or black, man or woman. And may God help you.

JUDGE HUNT,

AND

The Right of Trial by Jury.

By JOHN HOOKER, Hartford, Conn.

The following article was intended for publication in a magazine, but the writer kindly contributed it for publication in this pamphlet.

In the recent trial of Susan B. Anthony for voting, (illegally, as was claimed, on the ground that as a woman she had no right to vote—a point which we do not propose to consider,) the course of Judge Hunt, in taking the case from the jury, and ordering a verdict of guilty to be entered up, was so remarkable, so contrary to all rules of law, and so subversive of the system of jury trials in criminal cases, that it should not be allowed to pass without an emphatic protest on the part of every public journal that values our liberties.

Let us first of all see precisely what were the facts. Miss Anthony was charged with having knowingly voted, without lawful right to vote, at the Congressional election in the eighth ward of the City of Rochester, in the State of New York, in November, 1872. The Act of Congress under which the prosecution was brought provides that, "If, at any election for representative or delegate in the Congress of the United States, any person shall knowingly personate and vote, or attempt to vote, in the name of any other person, whether living, dead or fictitious, or vote more than once at the same election for any candidate for the same office, or vote at a place where he may not be lawfully entitled to vote, or vote without having a lawful right to vote, every such person shall be deemed guilty of a crime," &c.

The trial took place at Canandaigua, in the State of New York, in the Circuit Court of the United States, before Judge Hunt, of the Supreme Court of the United States.

The defendant pleaded not guilty—thus putting the Government upon the proof of their entire case, admitting, however, that she was a woman, but admitting nothing more.

The only evidence that she voted at all, and that, if at all, she voted for a representative in Congress, offered on the part of the government, was, that she handed four bits of paper, folded in the form of ballots, to the inspectors, to be placed in the voting boxes. There was nothing on the outside of these papers to indicate what they were, and the contents were not known to the witnesses nor to the inspectors. There were six ballot boxes, and each elector had the right to cast six ballots.

This evidence would undoubtedly warrant the conclusion that Miss Anthony voted for a Congressional representative, the fact probably appearing, although the papers before the writer do not show it, that one of the supposed ballots was placed by her direction in the box for votes for Members of Congress. The facts are thus minutely stated, not at all for the purpose of questioning their sufficiency, but to show how entirely it was a question of fact, and therefore a question for the jury.

Upon this evidence Judge Hunt directed the clerk to enter up a verdict of guilty. The counsel for the defendant interposed, but without effect, the judge closing the discussion by saying, " Take the verdict, Mr. Clerk." The clerk then said, " Gentlemen of the jury, hearken to your verdict, as the Court has recorded it. You say you find the defendant guilty of the offence whereof she stands indicted, and so say you all." To this the jury made no response, and were immediately after dismissed.

It is stated in one of the public papers, by a person present at the trial, that immediately after the dismissal of the jury, one of the jurors said to him that that was not his verdict, nor that of the rest, and that if he could have spoken he should have answered " Not guilty," and that other jurors would have sustained him in it. The writer has no authority for this statement, beyond the letter mentioned. The juror, of course, had a right, when the verdict was read by the clerk, to declare that it was not his verdict, but it is not strange, perhaps, that an ordinary juror, with no time to consider, or to consult with his fellows, and probably ignorant of his rights, and in awe of the Court, should have failed to assert himself at such a moment.

Probably the assumption by the judge that Miss Anthony in fact voted, did her no real injustice, as it was a notorious fact that she did vote, and claimed the right to do so. But all this made it no less an usurpation for the judge to take the case from the jury, and order a verdict of guilty to be entered up without consulting them.

There was, however, a real injustice done her by the course of the judge, inasmuch as the mere fact of her voting, and voting unlawfully, was not enough for her conviction. It is a perfectly settled rule of law that there must exist an intention to do an illegal act, to make an act a crime. It is, of course, not necessary that a person perpetrating a crime should have an actual knowledge of a certain law which forbids the act, but he must have a criminal intent. Thus, if one is charged with theft, and admits the taking of the property, which is clearly proved to have belonged to another, it is yet a good defence that he really believed that he had a right to take it, or that he took it by mistake. Just so in a case where, as sometimes occurs, the laws regulating the right to vote in a State are of doubtful meaning, and a voter is uncertain whether he has a right to vote in one town or another, and, upon taking advice from good counsel, honestly makes up his mind that he has a right to vote in the town of A. In this belief he applies to the registrars of that town, who upon the statement of the facts, are of the opinion that he has a right to vote there, and place his name upon the list, and on election day he votes there without objection. Now, if he should be prosecuted for illegal voting, it would not be enough that he acknowledged the fact of voting, and that the judge was of the opinion that his view of the law was wrong. There would remain another and most vital question in the case, and that is, did he intend to vote unlawfully? Now, precisely the wrong that would be done to the voter in the case we are supposing, by the judge ordering a verdict of guilty to be entered up, was done by that course in Miss Anthony's case. She thoroughly believed that she had a right to vote. In addition to this she had consulted one of the ablest lawyers in Western New York, who gave it as his opinion that she had a right to vote, and who testified on the trial that he had given her that advice. The Act of Congress upon which the prosecution was founded uses the term "knowingly,"—"shall knowingly vote or attempt to vote in the name of any other person, or more than once at the same election for any candidate for the same office, or vote at a place where he may not be lawfully entitled to vote, or without having a lawful right to vote." Here most manifestly the term "knowingly" does not apply to the mere *act* of voting. It is hardly possible that a man should vote, and not know the fact that he is voting. The statute will bear no possible construction but that which makes the term "knowingly" apply to the *illegality* of the act. Thus, "shall knowingly vote without having a lawful right to vote," can only mean, shall vote knowing that there is no lawful right to vote. This being so, there was manifestly a most vital question beyond that of the fact of voting, and of the conclusion of the judge that the voting was illegal, viz., did Miss Anthony vote, knowing that she had no right to vote.

Now, many people will say that Miss Anthony ought to have known that she had no right to vote, and will perhaps regard it as an audacious attempt for mere effect, to assert a right that she might think she ought to have, but could not really have believed that she had. But whatever degree of credit her claim to have acted honestly in the matter is entitled to, whether to much, or little, or none, it was entirely a question for the jury, and they alone could pass upon it. The judge had no right even to express an opinion on the subject to the jury, much less to instruct them upon it, and least of all to order a verdict of guilty without consulting them.

There seems to have been an impression, as the writer infers from various notices of the matter in the public papers, that the case had resolved itself into a pure question of law. Thus, a legal correspondent of one of our leading religious papers, in defending the course of Judge Hunt, says: "There was nothing before the Court but a pure question of law. Miss Anthony violated the law of the State intentionally and deliberately, as she openly avowed, and when brought to trial her only defence was that the law was unconstitutional. Here was nothing whatever to go to the jury." And again he says: "In jury trials all questions of law are decided by the judge." This writer is referred to only as expressing what are supposed to be the views of many others.

To show, however, how entirely incorrect is this assumption of fact, I insert here the written points submitted by Miss Anthony's counsel to the Court, for its instruction to the jury.

First—That if the defendant, at the time of voting, believed that she had a right to vote, and voted in good faith in that belief, she is not guilty of the offence charged.

Second—In determining the question whether she did or did not believe that she had a right to vote, the jury may take into consideration, as bearing upon that question, the advice which she received from the counsel to whom she applied.

Third—That they may also take into consideration, as bearing upon the same question, the fact that the inspectors considered the question, and came to the conclusion that she had a right to vote.

Fourth—That the jury have a right to find a general verdict of guilty or not guilty, as they shall believe that she has or has not been guilty of the offense prescribed in the statute.

This certainly makes it clear that the question was not "a pure question of law," and that there was "something to go to the jury." And this would be so, even if, as that writer erroneously supposes, Miss Anthony had openly avowed before the Court that she voted.

But even if this point be wholly laid out of the case, and it had been conceded that Miss Anthony had knowingly violated the law, if she should be proved to have voted at all, so that the only questions before the Court were, first—whether she had voted as charged, and secondly—whether the law forbade her voting; and if in this state of the case a hundred witnesses had been brought by the government, to testify that she had "openly avowed" in their presence that she had voted, so that practically the question of her having voted was proved beyond all possible question, still, the judge would have no right to order a verdict of guilty. The proof that she voted would still be *evidence*, and *mere evidence*, and a judge has no power whatever to deal with evidence. He can deal only with the law of the case, and the jury alone can deal with the facts.

But we will go further than this. We will suppose that in New York, as in some of the States, a defendant in a criminal case is allowed to testify, and that Miss Anthony had gone upon the stand as a witness, and had stated distinctly and unequivocally that she did in fact vote as charged. We must not forget that, if this had actually occurred, she would at the same time have stated that she voted in the full belief that she had a right to vote, and that she was advised by eminent counsel that she had such right; a state of the case which we have before referred to as presenting a vital question of fact for the jury, and which excludes the possibility of the case being legally dealt with by the judge alone; but this point we are laying out of the case in the view we are now taking of it. We will suppose that Miss Anthony not only testified that she voted in fact, but also that she had no belief that she had any right to vote;

making a case where, if the Court should hold as matter of law that she had no right to vote, there would seem to be no possible verdict for the jury to bring in but that of "guilty."

Even in this case, which would seem to resolve itself as much as possible into a mere question of law, there is yet no power whatever on the part of the judge to order a verdict of guilty, but it rests entirely in the judgment and conscience of the jury what verdict they will bring in. They may act unwisely and unconscientiously, perhaps by mere favoritism, or a weak sympathy, or prejudice, or on any other indefensible ground; but yet they have entire *power* over the matter. It is for them finally to say what their verdict shall be, and the judge has no power beyond that of instruction upon the law involved in the case.

The proposition laid down by the writer before referred to, that "in jury trials all questions of law are decided by the judge," is not unqualifiedly true. It is so in civil causes, but in criminal causes it has been holden by many of our best courts that the jury are judges of the law as well as of the facts. Pages could be filled with authorities in support of this proposition. The courts do hold, however, that the judges are to *instruct* the jury as to the law, and that it is their duty to take the law as thus laid down. But it has never been held that if the jury assume the responsibility of holding a prisoner not guilty in the face of a charge from the judge that required a verdict of guilty, where the question was wholly one of law, they had not full power to do it.

The question is one ordinarily of little practical importance, but it here helps to make clear the very point we are discussing. Here the judge laid down the law, correctly, we will suppose, certainly in terms that left the jury no doubt as to what he meant; and here, by all the authorities, the jury ought, as a matter of proper deference in one view, or of absolute duty in the other, to have adopted the view of the law given them by the judge. But it was in either case the *jury only* who could apply the law to the case. The judge could *instruct*, but the jury only could *apply the instruction.* That is, the instruction of the judge, no matter how authoritative we may regard it, could find its way to the defendant *only through the verdict of the jury.*

It is only where the confession of facts is *matter of record,* (that is, where the plea filed or recorded in the case *admits* them), that the judge can enter up a judgment without the finding of a jury. Thus, if the defendant pleads "guilty," there is no need of a jury finding him so. If, however, he pleads "not guilty," then, no matter how overwhelming is the testimony against him on the trial, no matter if a hundred witnesses prove his admission of all the facts, the whole is not legally decisive like a plea of guilty; but the question still remains a question of fact, and the jury alone can determine what the verdict shall be. In other words, it is no less a question of fact for the reason that the evidence is all one way and overwhelming, or that the defendant has in his testimony admitted all the facts against himself.

The writer has intended this article for general rather than professional readers, and has therefore not encumbered it with authorities; but he has stated only rules and principles that are well established and familiar to all persons practising in our courts of law.

This case illustrates an important defect in the law with regard to the revision of verdicts and judgments in the United States Circuit Court. In almost all other courts, an application for a new trial on the ground of erroneous rulings by the judge, is made to a higher and independent tribunal. In this court, however, an application for a new trial is addressed to and decided by the same judge who tried the case, and whose erroneous rulings are complained of. Such a motion was made and argued by Miss Anthony's counsel before Judge Hunt, who refused to grant a new trial. Thus it was Judge Hunt alone who was to decide whether Judge Hunt was wrong. It is manifest that the opportunity for securing justice even before the most honest of judges, would be somewhat less than before an entirely distinct tribunal, as the judge would be prejudiced in favor of his own opinion, and the best and most learned of judges are human and fallible; while if a judge is disposed to be unfair, it is perfectly easy for him to suppress all attempts of a party injured by his decision to set it aside.

The only remedy for a party thus wronged is by an appeal to the public. Such an appeal, as a friend of justice and of the law, without regard to Miss Anthony's case in any other aspect, the writer makes in this article. The public, thus the only appellate tribunal, should willingly listen to such a case, and pass its own supreme and decisive judgment upon it.

The writer cannot but regard Judge Hunt's course as not only irregular as a matter of law, but a very dangerous encroachment on the right of every person accused to be tried by a jury. It is by yielding to such encroachments that liberties are lost.

www.ingramcontent.com/pod-product-compliance
Lightning Source LLC
LaVergne TN
LVHW011203110826
845150LV00006B/1306
* 9 7 8 1 4 2 5 5 1 8 2 8 8 *